Why Marijuana Should Be Legal

Why Marijuana Should Be Legal

by Ed Rosenthal & Steve Kubby
with S. Newhart

RUNNING PRESS
PHILADELPHIA • LONDON

First published by Thunder's Mouth Press in 1996

9   8   7   6   5   4
Digit on the right indicates the number of this printing

Library of Congress Cataloging-in-Publication Data is available

ISBN-13: 978-1-56025-481-2
ISBN-10: 0-1-56025-481-5

Book design by Simon M. Sullivan

This book may be ordered by mail from the publisher.
Please include $2.50 for postage and handling.
But try your bookstore first!

Running Press Book Publishers
2300 Chestnut Street
Philadelphia, PA 19103-4371

Visit us on the web!
www.runningpress.com

To Jeff Jones and Debbie Goldsberry,
New Grist for the Mill

Acknowledgments

This book is the result of the efforts of some very dedicated people. We would like to thank them all for their efforts. Of course, as the authors, we take complete responsibility for any errors or oversights in information.

The people at Thunder's Mouth Press for their support of this book.

Jane Klein helped to materialize this book through her tireless efforts at all stages of its development. Her skills and talents were fully exploited.

Michelle Kubby contributed her insights and suggestions.

Jerry Mandel helped with the fact and source checking. He persevered through a tedious, technical task.

William Dolphin for his excellent editorial recommendations and computer assistance.

Julia Browne for her friendly administrative help.

Marijuana advocacy groups compiled many of the statistics we used. We would like to thank them for attempting to make this a better society.

Contents

Introduction ix

1
Preserving Our Constitutional Rights 1

2
Criminal Innocents 15

3
Economic Costs 25

4
Health Effects 35

5
Hemp: Industrial Applications 43

6
Medical Applications 49

7
National Security 61

8
Sociological Aspects 71

9
Why Marijuana Isn't Legal 85

10
How to Legalize Marijuana 107

11
Ed Rosenthal on His Arrest 121

Appendix 1
*Proposition 215: California Medical
Use of Marijuana Initiative Statute 127*

Appendix 2
Acronyms and Abbreviations 129

Notes 133

Introduction

Marijuana is a part of American culture. Over 65 million Americans use it either occasionally or regularly. However, social acceptance has not led to a reduction of penalties for its use. Nearly 800,000 users get arrested each year.[1] In the last thirty years, over 10 million Americans have been arrested on marijuana charges.[2] In some cases, people are serving up to thirty years for simple possession.

This book was written to focus on the real issue involved in the marijuana controversy: Which is more harmful to society, marijuana or the marijuana laws?

Before we make a reasoned decision about marijuana, we should weigh the effects marijuana has on society against the effects the marijuana laws have. If marijuana is more harmful to society than the laws, then the laws should be retained. If the laws are more harmful than the substance, the laws should be changed.

There are several reasons why marijuana remains illegal. Most importantly, it is a political football kicked around by a number of self-serving groups. Some of these groups perceive marijuana as a threat to the national fabric, tearing families apart and causing us to abandon our traditional values. Parents have always expressed these concerns, but they are not legitimate areas of legislation.

There are groups that have more practical reasons for keeping marijuana illegal. The most powerful of these are the combined law-enforcement-judiciary-penal systems. This group sees the elimination of marijuana laws as a threat to their jobs.

Another interest group includes the scientists whose marijuana research is funded by the government. If marijuana were legalized, these researchers would lose millions of dollars in grants intended to prove the deleterious effects of the herb. Recently, many of these same researchers have changed their opinions as they see development opportunities and hard evidence supporting marijuana's medical uses.

Two other related and very influential groups are the liquor lobby and pharmaceutical companies, whose spending is clouded in secrecy. Marijuana legalization would cut deeply into their profits by making available a competing product that can be produced with relative ease by anyone with access to a plot of land. The drug companies want control, rather than just a ban, for they know the medicinal benefits of marijuana. They have attempted to substitute synthetic derivatives for the raw herb, because the raw herb cannot be patented, meaning they can't make money from it.

Every year, thousands of marijuana cases are prosecuted for political reasons. Politicians use the marijuana issue to scare the voters. Marijuana prohibition has even reached presidential politics. Clinton swore that he "smoked but didn't inhale."

Antilegalization groups argue that if marijuana were legalized, there would be no way to regulate its use by or sales to minors. This is an absurd argument. Society has a better chance of controlling behavior using civil regulation than banning it and removing it from regulatory control. In addition, opponents cite marijuana's supposed threat to health. They postulate that if it is harmful, then it should remain illegal. Although the scientific community is divided over whether the herb does have negative health effects, opponents maintain that until absolute certainty of its benign nature is established, marijuana should be banned. They don't ask, is the cure worse than the problem?

Many people are opposed to legalization simply because they perceive users as undesirable: minorities, deviants, and other unwholesome types. Law-enforcement officials seem to use marijuana laws as a means of selective oppression. Today these laws are often used in the same way that vagrancy laws were used to clean up the streets (until they were found to be unconstitutional).

As we shall show, antilegalization policies, while well meaning, are in fundamental conflict with the American concept of liberty and the pursuit of happiness. Our Constitution guarantees us these rights. The marijuana laws affect millions of people, weakening our frail democracy with an escalating drug war: more police, more prosecutions, and more citizens in jail.

The damage to the physical and mental health of millions of Americans as a result of arrest, incarceration, lost property, and humiliation are far more serious than any medical damage ever reported from the use of marijuana. The dangers of incarceration, especially violence and rape, have been well documented. Only the most virulent dogmatist could possibly believe that smoking a joint is more harmful than the terrors and heartbreak that are routine in prison life.

While the government claims marijuana should continue to be banned because of health issues, the marijuana laws have hurt millions of people. To claim that an issue that is so controversial is solely health related requires an ostrich-like view of society. The "health issue" is just an excuse, not the real reason for its continued criminalization.

The government has no right to determine how we think—that is a basic tenet of our democracy. Marijuana affects the way a person perceives reality.[3] Many people who have used it can describe important insights they had while high, and they certainly believe that marijuana facilitated the thought process. Thus, marijuana laws are the ultimate form of thought control, directing not only what we might think but also how we might think. Few politicians are willing to seriously discuss the individual's right to choose a process of consciousness.

It is our opinion, of course, that marijuana should be legal. But the legacy of misinformation from previous eras of marijuana hysteria makes it difficult to dispassionately examine the societal effects of marijuana and the laws against it.

We have attempted to provide a clearer comparison of the effects of marijuana versus the effects of marijuana laws. To do so, we will examine both from eight different perspectives: constitutional, criminal, economic, health, industrial, medical, national security, and sociological. From the standpoints of logic, costs, and benefits, our discussion will reveal that legalizing marijuana and creating a system of civil regulation would serve the best interests of the country.

Why Marijuana Should Be Legal

1

Preserving Our Constitutional Rights

While visiting Morocco in 1982, my guide and I hopped in a taxi to go from the Rif Mountains to Casablanca. The driver thought I was a smuggler and drove me straight into the local police station, where my luggage was searched. Coming down from the mountains, I encountered two more police stops. On both occasions I was singled out for search because I was of European descent.

Soon thereafter, I wrote a column saying how lucky we are in the United States to live under the protection of the Bill of Rights. I compared what happened to me in Morocco with the constitutional protections that Americans are guaranteed, specifically under the Fourth Amendment, which prohibits police searches without a warrant.

However, in 1996, the Supreme Court shot holes in the Fourth Amendment. In the case of *Whren v. U.S.*, the high court ruled that police can stop a car on a pretense and then search it on the slightest suspicion—sort of a drug exemption to the Constitution.

This had a chilling effect on me during a recent trip to New York City. My host and I were traveling downtown on Fifth Avenue by taxi. Traffic was backed up. The driver tried to take an alternate route, but the police blocked the side streets. The traffic narrowed to one lane and passed through a phalanx of officers who looked over the passengers and contents of each car, pulling over certain motorists for further inspection. We weren't stopped.

As we drove away from the roadblock, my host told me that anyone the police didn't like was likely to be pulled over: Rastafarians, Deadheads, blacks, Hispanics, cars sporting political stickers, messy cars, even foreign cars. (In the 1960s, Detroit police regularly stopped people driving foreign cars, doing their part to protect the domestic auto industry.)

Until *Whren v. U.S.*, a citizen had the right to say, "I'm sorry, officer, but I am not going to give you consent to search my car, and unless I'm under arrest, I intend to leave right now." Without probable cause—seeing or smelling marijuana or some other prohibited article—the officer would have had no right to search the citizen's car.

This frightening expansion of the state's power is a direct result of the drug wars. Our freedom just isn't worth compromising for the impossible goal of limiting the use of drugs by consenting adults.

The Bill of Rights specifically asserts that the government can't intrude upon rights in certain areas, such as speech, religion, or search and seizure. We came together as a society not to restrict the rights of the individual, but to secure the rights of all. These amendments to the Constitution don't place limits on what an individual may do; instead, they limit what the government is allowed to do, keeping it a servant of "We, the People." We claim to be a diverse, pluralistic, multicultural society, yet under marijuana prohibition, our government has adopted zero tolerance for people whose lifestyle is not acceptable to those in power.

The marijuana laws and their enforcement violate the First, Fourth, Fifth, Sixth, Eighth, Ninth, and Tenth Amendments. With so many bad laws in effect, many people are tempted to dismiss violations of the Bill of Rights as part of the mess. However, the Constitution and the Bill of Rights are the supreme law of the land. No one, not even the government, is above the Constitution.

The First Amendment tells the federal government to keep its hands off certain rights:

> Congress shall make no law respecting an establishment of religion, or prohibiting the free exercise thereof; or abridging the freedom of speech, or of the press; or the right of the people peaceably to assemble, and to petition the government for a redress of grievances.

The government is not to make any law about religion, speech, press, or assembly. In spite of this, the current government holds that only religions that conform to its standards are legal. Marijuana has been used for religious purposes for thousands of years.[1] Today it is used in Hindu, Buddhist, and various tribal celebrations. During holiday periods, some higher-caste Hindu men are required to drink bhang, a cannabis-milk infusion, to bring them closer to Shiva. Some newer religions also use marijuana sacramentally.

Stephen's Farm in Tennessee (the largest religious commune in the United States), the Rastafarians, and the Ethiopian Zionist Coptic Church are among the New Age or newly organized religions that do so. In 1996, the Rastafarians even obtained a court ruling granting them the right to use pot in their religious ceremonies.[2] However, separate charges as "drug kingpins" were filed against the Rastafarians, and convictions were obtained against them.

The First Amendment also guarantees freedom of speech. However, the FBI and Drug Enforcement Agency (DEA) use selective arrests and prosecution to intimidate pro-marijuana advocates.[3]

Regardless of their personal beliefs, these government employees are violating our democratic and constitutional right to free speech and religious freedom.

The Fourth Amendment grants us the right to privacy and security against unreasonable searches and seizures:

> The right of the people to be secure in their persons, houses, papers and effects against unreasonable searches and seizures, shall not be violated and no warrants shall issue, but upon probable cause, supported by oath or affirmation, and particularly describing the place to be searched, and the persons or things to be seized.

We are not supposed to have to worry about searches and seizures, yet under the marijuana laws, the government conducts searches all the time on the slightest of evidence. According to attorney Richard Glen Boire: "In addition to taking your cash and your car, the state and federal governments can take your home and real property. Under federal law, cultivation of marijuana is a felony punishable by more than one year in prison, so the federal government can seize your home and real property even if a single cannabis plant is found on the property. Even if the marijuana was solely for your own personal use and not for sale, it can form the basis for property forfeiture under federal law."[4]

Recent Supreme Court rulings have eroded our freedom further by allowing warrantless searches during traffic stops and searches conducted "in good faith" but with bad warrants. Some people, including a few of the Supreme Court justices, argue that such extreme measures are necessary to create a drug-free society. When police can randomly harass motorists in search of contraband, then the society we are creating is one where freedom and democracy are illegal. One bumper sticker put it succinctly: "Free or Drug-Free: You Can't Have Both."

The Fifth Amendment grants citizens important rights if they are accused of a crime, and specifically forbids the government from depriving us of property without due process of law:

> No person shall be held to answer for a capital, or otherwise infamous crime, unless on a presentment or indictment of a grand jury, except in cases arising in the land or naval forces, or in the militia, when in actual service in time of war or public danger; nor shall any person be subject for the same offense to be twice put in jeopardy of life or limb; nor shall be compelled in any criminal case to be a witness against himself, nor be deprived of life, liberty, or property, without due process of law; nor shall private property be taken for public use without just compensation.

This amendment is crystal clear, yet the government violates it all the time. The federal government's tax and police agencies are notorious for seizing property without due process—nearly $1 billion in the year 1999.[5] In 80 percent of cases, property is seized without charges being filed.[6] Most of the seized property goes directly to the police departments and informants, creating a frightening situation where police raise money by raiding private citizens.[7]

Drug testing in criminal cases clearly violates the Fifth Amendment protection against self-incrimination, but the Supreme Court has ruled that random testing is acceptable. Even the section dealing with immunity has been emasculated with "use immunity," which states that the government can prosecute you for crimes you testified

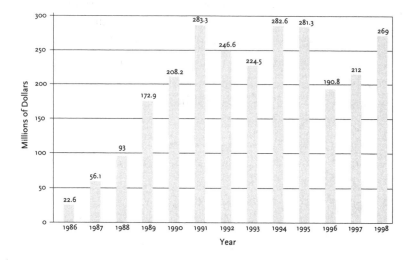

Police Receive $250 Million Bonus for Asset Seizures. Through the "Equitable Sharing Program," the federal government can give the local or state cops up to 80% of a civil asset seizure when the conduct leading to the seizure broke a federal law and allowed for forfeiture under federal law; in other words, in drug-related seizures. As a result, around half of all civil asset seizures go directly to the coffers of the cops who seized the goods. The feds keep the other half. Very often this money is not counted in figuring local police budgets. Source: Adapted from Drug Policy Foundation Asset Forfeiture Briefing, 1999, which cited data from the *Annual Report of the Dept. of Justice Asset Forfeiture Program,* fiscal year 1996, p. 3; estimates for FY 1997 and 1998 taken from *National Drug Control Strategy: Budget Summary* (1997, 1998) p. 98, 106. The 1994–1998; figures include data from *Treasury Forfeiture Fund Annual Report* (1994-1998).

to under immunity if the prosecution develops the evidence "independently." In addition, citizens are routinely prosecuted for drug crimes by both state and federal governments, thus subjecting them to punishment twice for the same crime.

The Sixth Amendment guarantees the right to speedy public trials:

> In all criminal prosecutions, the accused shall enjoy the right
> to a speedy and public trial, by an impartial jury of the state

and district wherein the crime shall have been committed, which district shall have been previously ascertained by law, and to be informed of the nature and cause of the accusation; to be confronted with the witnesses against him; to have compulsory process for obtaining witnesses in his favor, and to have the assistance of counsel for his defense.

Because the war on pot has packed our jails with ordinary citizens, the entire criminal justice system has become a mockery. Plea bargaining and drug-diversion programs are used to subvert the judicial process and help unclog the mess caused by all the pot busts. The more packed the courts, the greater the likelihood of plea bargaining. In 1980, when 5,006 persons charged with violating federal drug laws faced a trial, 69 percent pleaded guilty or *nolo contendere;* in 2000, five times as many persons faced such federal charges, but 94 percent of the defendants chose not to contest the case.[8]

People who are accused of marijuana crimes and who "accept responsibility," rather than asserting their right to trial, are promised lighter sentences under federal guidelines. Such perversions of our judicial process are far more serious threats than any drug. For instance, Bryan Epis, a medical-marijuana provider, was offered a plea bargain of four and a half years, which he did not accept. He was found guilty by a jury and sentenced to ten years in federal prison. In comparison, the Symbionese Liberation Army members who pleaded guilty to murdering a bank customer in a botched robbery were sentenced to less than eight years.

Defendants find it hard to obtain witnesses because they refuse to testify without immunity, which the prosecution will not provide. The use of "confidential informants" also denies defendants the right to confront their accusers. Worst of all, the Supreme Court has ruled that defendants do not have the right to use a "medical necessity" defense in federal courts. This keeps the jury from considering the context. In federal cases, juries are kept ignorant of the complete set of facts.[9]

Keith Alden, a Sonoma County medical-marijuana provider, declined a plea bargain, opting for trial. Judge Martin Jenkins rigorously excluded any mention of medicine, illness, medical-marijuana, or California's medical-marijuana proposition in the court proceedings. When medical, marijuana patient Allen McFarlane was called to testify, he was reprimanded for mentioning persons with AIDS and cancer, even though he is a patient himself. The judge dismissed the jury and warned McFarlane against incriminating himself.[10]

When the jury reconvened, McFarlane invoked the Fifth Amendment, but his comment that he did so under threat provoked a second reprimand from the court. The court's reprimands, combined with the exclusion of medical-marijuana information, silenced McFarlane's testimony. Alden was found guilty on a cultivation charge. His sentence was downgraded due to various extenuating factors,[11] but a second set of charges filed against Alden for cultivating while on probation may result in a twenty-year mandatory minimum sentence.[12]

The Seventh Amendment guarantees the right to trial by jury:

> In suits at common law, where the value in controversy shall exceed twenty dollars, the right of trial by jury shall be preserved, and no fact tried by a jury, shall be otherwise reexamined in any court of the United States, than according to the rules of the common law.

Trial by jury is so important that the founding fathers gave juries the constitutional right to acquit if they think the law is wrong. This right to nullify laws through the actions of a jury is one of the greatest weapons that citizens have to oppose bad laws. The founders understood that even the best of governments can pass bad laws and that juries of common citizens must have the right to judge both the accused and the law.

Marijuana defendants have the right to a jury trial, but the courts use threats of punishment to pressure defendants into pleading to a charge. Judges and district attorneys abhor jury trials, and they stop at nothing to pressure people into giving up their constitutional right to one. "Drug courts" are being used to intimidate defendants. In these courts there is a presumption of guilt, and the defendant is asked to waive all rights.

The Eighth Amendment specifically prohibits excessive bail, fines, and punishment:

> Excessive bail shall not be required, nor excessive fines imposed, nor cruel and unusual punishments inflicted. Bail for drug defendants is usually much higher than for others. When I was arrested in February 2002 for assisting medical-marijuana patients, the cash retainer was set at $200,000 on $500,000 bond. This is not unusual.

The founding fathers would be shocked at the excessive bails, fines, and punishments inflicted for violation of our drug laws. People are being jailed for twenty-five years, without the possibility of parole, for having a joint. Their homes and property are being seized because they are growing a plant. Surely this flouts the Eighth Amendment.

Prison for life without parole (LWOP) is not unusual for "serious" marijuana offenses. Murderers and rapists rarely get LWOP, but marijuana entrepreneurs can expect LWOP, especially if they refuse to become government informants. Sending people to prison for the rest of their lives for growing marijuana is not only a clear violation of the Constitution but tramples human rights as badly as anything going on in the most despotic and totalitarian countries.

The Ninth Amendment reserves to every American all rights not considered in the Bill of Rights:

> The enumeration in the Constitution, of certain rights, shall not be construed to deny or disparage others retained by the people.

The Ninth Amendment is unequivocal—just because the Constitution defines only certain rights doesn't mean rights that haven't been defined can be taken away. Certainly none of the authors of the Bill of Rights gave a thought to including the right to get high or to use drugs, because those rights weren't being threatened. Anyone could grow or buy marijuana at that time. It wasn't until 1937–139 years after the government was organized—that the feds started to "tax" marijuana. They decided it would be unconstitutional to make it illegal, so taxation was used as a method of control. It wasn't criminalized until 1967.

That We, the People, have rights that can never be taken by the government is further solidified by the Tenth Amendment:

> The powers not delegated to the United States by the Constitution, nor prohibited by it to the states, are reserved to the states respectively, or to the people.

The Tenth Amendment explicitly states that any legal powers not granted by the Constitution to the federal government and not prohibited by the state governments are reserved to the people and the states that represent them.

The Tenth Amendment left intrastate commerce to the regulation of the individual states. However, since California passed Proposition 215, the medical-marijuana initiative, the federal government has interfered with California's internal affairs, just as it has with the other states whose voters and legislatures have seen fit to legalize medical use of marijuana. The federal government, which was supposed to have specifically limited powers, has now become so powerful that it leads the world in prisons, sting operations, secret police, paid informants, aerial surveillance, wiretaps, urine testing, searches, and seizures.

THE CONSTITUTION:
VOID WHERE PROHIBITED BY LAW!

Here are some of the unconstitutional things that the government may do to you if you are convicted, or even just accused, of a marijuana crime.

Forfeiture of Assets

You could lose everything you own if you are simply accused of a marijuana crime. Eighty percent of the people whose assets are seized by the federal government under drug laws are never formally charged with a crime. The government sometimes acknowledges that the owners were innocent—the property was guilty.

Suspension of Driver's License

Many states now mandate a six-month driver's license suspension if you're convicted of possession of any amount of marijuana.

Revocation of Benefits

Student loans and public housing are two of the multitude of federal benefits that may be taken away from you if you're convicted of a marijuana crime. Over 43,000 of the student applicants for federal grants, work-study programs, or subsidized loans were rejected because of a prior conviction for drugs.[13] Given the disproportionately high drug-arrest rates among young African-Americans and Hispanics, one would expect minority students to be especially affected by the revocation of benefits.

Loss of Custody

If you're convicted of some marijuana offenses, the state can force you to surrender custody of your children.

Loss of Livelihood

A number of states revoke professional licenses of convicted marijuana offenders. This affects not only doctors and lawyers, but also state-licensed plumbers, beauticians, educators, and so on. If you're in the military, expect an automatic discharge.

Jail Time

Courts determine the penalties for possession of a firearm by pot smokers if the firearm is used "in relation to any drug-trafficking crime." For example, if you're arrested for possession of marijuana "with intent to distribute" and you have a loaded rifle in the room where the pot is stored, you could be sentenced to a mandatory five-year prison term for possession of the rifle. This penalty is in addition to those that apply to the marijuana crime itself.

Additional Taxes and Fines

The Internal Revenue Service may audit you if you are convicted of a marijuana offense. Many states have very high "taxes" on pot, and assess fines of as much as several million dollars against those convicted of marijuana crimes.

No citizen of any other country has ever faced such a formidable array of high-tech surveillance, secret police, prison camps, and well-paid informants as the marijuana users of the U.S. We are peered at and listened to by cameras and microphones, as we walk down our streets, ride in our cars, or even sit in our houses. We are photographed, fingerprinted, urine tested, lie detected, and body searched because our own government has decided that citizens who consume the herb marijuana are criminals.

As private citizens living under a hostile government, we have little more to protect ourselves with than a document drafted over 200 years ago that guarantees our rights and freedoms. The Bill of Rights was created for all Americans, not just those who agree to live according to the beliefs and values of those in power. The Bill of Rights is supposed to allow all Americans to live according to their own creeds, as free citizens entitled to "life, liberty, and the pursuit of happiness." The founders intended Americans to be a free people, protected from horrors like secret police, warrantless searches, seizures, forfeitures, and excessive punishments.

Until the marijuana laws are repealed, our freedom will continue to be violated by the same police and public officials who are sworn to uphold and defend the Constitution against all enemies, foreign and domestic. The long-haired, freedom-loving patriots who founded this country would never have tolerated the current marijuana laws—nor should we.

2

Criminal Innocents

On April 29, 1996, amid media fanfare, then President Clinton and his drug czar, General McCaffrey, unveiled a ten-year antidrug program involving the use of military assets against American citizens. This program was a complete failure.

Not since the Civil War has any president allowed the American military to be used against its own citizens. The Clinton program called for a record $15.1 billion a year to initiate a "decade-long commitment" to reduce drug use in America. That was a whopping 1,000 percent increase in antidrug money over the $1.5 billion budget of a decade before. McCaffrey admitted there was no guarantee these efforts would be any more successful in eradicating drugs than the previous ones. Although arrests rates nearly doubled nationally, marijuana use increased.[1] The program was destined to fail —redoubling efforts in a misconceived project cannot turn it around. The federal War on Drugs budget first topped $1 billion in 1981. It steadily increased during the next twelve years of the Reagan and elder Bush presidencies to an enormous $12 billion; and it increased to $18 billion under Clinton's eight-year presidency. [2]

Under President G. W. Bush, the war on pot has escalated again.

He has boosted the federal drug budget another billion, to $19.2 for 2003.[3] The new drug czar, John P. Walters, has been given extraordinary powers and facilities, including military spy planes and DEA "classified programs," to wage war against American citizens who use pot.

The Bush administration is just as contemptuous of the American people as its predecessors. Even though the voters have repeatedly shown support for medical marijuana, Drug Czar Walters and DEA Administrator Asa Hutchinson have focused on arresting medical-marijuana patients and their providers. This campaign will succeed only in alienating the public.

Since their inception, the nation's antimarijuana laws have been absolutely ineffective in halting marijuana use. When marijuana prohibition was instituted in 1937, the government estimated that there were 55,000 users in the United States. Sixty-five years later, the estimate has exploded to 30 million—upwards of an eighth of the total adult population, a 5,000 percent increase. In 1994, there were 481,098 arrests for marijuana.[4] By 2000 there were 734,500.[5] Despite all these arrests, more Americans than ever use pot.[6]

In 1981, about 49 percent of the 196,000 people cited or arrested for marijuana were under twenty-one years old. This percentage has remained fairly constant since then.[7] For most of these youths, their pot bust is their first time in trouble with the law. After examining a sample of pre-1972 marijuana arrests, the National Commission on Marijuana and Drug Abuse (known as the Shafer Commission and established by Congress in 1970 to inquire into marijuana usage in the United States[8]) concluded that, "These [youthful] marijuana arrestees generally had no contact with law enforcement agencies prior to the marijuana arrest. The data suggest that the marijuana arrest constituted the initial experience with the criminal justice system, particularly among juveniles."[9]

Not only do marijuana arrests contribute to jail overcrowding, they

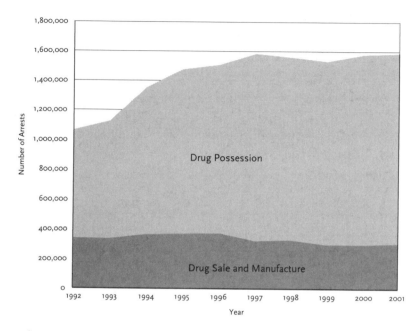

Police Target Users, Not Dealers. Arrests of dealers have been stable for over a decade. Possession arrests, on the other hand, rose from 1.1 million to 1.6 million, an increase of nearly 50 percent. This chart includes all drugs, but marijuana arrests follow the same trend. Source: Bureau of Justice Statistics, FBI Uniform Crime Reports, "Crime in the United States—2001."

also place the detainees in an unsavory environment where they meet and socialize with criminals, learn illegal trades, and are in personal danger. In testimony before the Senate Special Subcommittee on Alcoholism and Narcotics on September 18, 1969, Judge Charles W. Halleck of the District of Columbia Court of General Sessions explained why he no longer gave jail sentences to youthful marijuana offenders:

> If I send a [long-haired marijuana offender] to jail even for 30 days, Senator, he is going to be the victim of the most brutal type of homosexual, unnatural, perverted assaults and attacks that

you can imagine, and anybody who tells you it doesn't happen in that jail day in and day out is simply not telling you the truth. . . . How in God's name, Senator, can I send anybody to that jail knowing that? How can I send some poor young kid who gets caught by some zealous policeman who wants to make his record on a narcotics arrest? How can I send that kid to jail? I can't do it. So I put him on probation or I suspend the sentence and everybody says the judge doesn't care. The judge doesn't care about drugs, lets them all go. You simply can't treat these kinds of people like that.[10]

The situation in jails and prisons has deteriorated considerably since Judge Halleck made this statement thirty-three years ago. Certainly using marijuana is not as harmful as this prison experience.

Because of the official hysteria created by marijuana use, there is a serious question as to whether offenders can receive fair treatment in our criminal system. Two cases are examples of this.

Donnie Clark is from Myakka City, Florida, and he grew marijuana from 1979 until 1985, when local police arrested him. He was sentenced to probation and two years of house arrest. Donnie stopped growing marijuana after his arrest, although his sons and many of his friends still ran extensive cultivating operations.

In 1990, federal agents came to Myakka City and arrested twenty-eight people, including Donnie, for conspiracy to grow more than 1 million marijuana plants. The first two growers to be caught traded testimony for time and received three-year sentences. Donnie's son Duane, who had pioneered a new technique of growing in swamps, received ten years and his partner received eleven years. Donnie's other son, Gary, who also grew marijuana, received a seven-year sentence. Donnie had already served a state sentence for the marijuana he grew. Nevertheless, he was accused of being the ringleader and formally charged with conspiracy, which carries a life sentence.[11] He was the only defendant to take his case to trial. He was found guilty and received life imprisonment. He spent ten years behind bars before his presidential pardon in 2000.[12]

Roy Sharpnack is a fifty-five-year-old medical-marijuana user with Ménière's disease, an inner-ear disorder that causes severe attacks of dizziness, often accompanied by hearing loss or ringing in the ear. Sharpnack was helping to cultivate almost 1,000 plants for 100 verified medical-marijuana patients in El Dorado County, California. He followed California law by obtaining notarized medical authorization from doctors in the Sacramento area. Along with the other dispensary suppliers, Roy had acquired all of the necessary paperwork to protect himself under Proposition 215. When Roy was arrested along with a few others, the state of California declined to prosecute.[13]

Even though no interstate commerce was involved, the federal government pursued the case. Other defendants arrested at the same time pled to lesser charges or were freed after agreeing to cooperate. In 2002, Sharpnack was sentenced to just under five years. He has been denied the synthesized THC pill, Marinol, while in prison even though he has a prescription.[14]

For the vast majority of people who use pot, the use of a restricted substance is the only conscious illegal act they commit. Otherwise, they are productive, tax-paying citizens. But the marijuana laws make them fear the police in the course of ordinary living. Since the police do not have the confidence of a large portion of the citizenry, they have more difficulty doing their jobs. Were there no laws prohibiting marijuana use, these citizens would have much less fear of and hostility toward law enforcement. They would be much more helpful in criminal investigations.

Enforcing marijuana laws drains resources that should be properly used to fight violent crime. Nationwide, there were more arrests for marijuana than there were for arson, manslaughter, rape, stolen property, vandalism, and sex offenses combined.[15] Based on number of arrests, marijuana enforcement accounts for more than 10 percent of total police resources nationwide. The sheer number of marijuana violators overwhelms some law-enforcement agencies.

Marijuana laws lower the morale of law-enforcement agencies for reasons besides diversion of scarce resources. Many officers recognize that marijuana use is a benign activity and that enforcement generates hostility from otherwise law-abiding users. The Shafer Commission also recognized this problem:

> A majority of prosecutors agree that the existing marijuana laws do not deter people from initiating use, or users from using regularly or from transferring small amounts for little or no consideration. The law enforcement officers' work involving marijuana is totally in vain, accomplishing nothing but placing people in a confrontational path with the law. At the same time, law enforcement's credibility in the community is jeopardized.[16]

As with other banned substances from time immemorial, agencies charged with enforcing marijuana laws also have to deal with official corruption. Because of the high risk in the marijuana business, those involved in marijuana sales on a large basis often try to bribe police officers and other agents. Given the huge sums of money involved, some portion of the law-enforcement community will always be seduced.

It is virtually certain that one of the major profiteers is organized crime because of the black-market nature of the marijuana business. The most appropriate example is what happened under Prohibition in the 1920s and 1930s. Former small-time hoods were able to build great crime networks, eventually gaining so much strength that they infiltrated mainstream businesses. Now another source of untaxed, illicit profit—the imported marijuana trade—is adding to the wealth and power of organized crime. The more sophisticated government attempts at eradication become, the more risky and expensive the marijuana business will be. Small-time marijuana importers have quit the business and have been replaced by professional criminal organizations. This serves as encouragement for people to grow their own.

Officers and prosecuting attorneys enforcing laws against victimless crimes have problems in their work that officers investigating a crime against a person or property do not face. Police usually have a victim's full cooperation. But law-enforcement agents must use surreptitious means of obtaining evidence in marijuana cases. Covert police work is hostile to the concept of a free society because it entails the use of undercover agents, spies, informers, and entrapment. (Not coincidentally, evidence collected this way is often subjected to constitutional challenges based on illegal search or other technicalities.) Victims of this harassment are often forced to become informers, implicating friends and associates. While these methods may be good prosecution, they bode ill for society.

In order to discover criminal activity, police sometimes engage in illegal activities themselves. For example, while attempting to entrap a victim, the police sometimes deliver drugs that are eventually distributed.

The need to present evidence in the courtroom has led law enforcement and prosecutors to whittle away at the Bill of Rights. As mentioned in chapter 1, the Supreme Court has ruled that police can stop a car on a traffic pretense, then search it without a warrant. It also ruled that states have a right to close certain stores if they carry drug information as well as novelties.

The marijuana laws themselves cause crime and violence. People who earn a living from the marijuana trade have no police protection, and so are at the mercy of criminal elements. In some areas, this problem is out of control. Miami is notorious for drug-related violence; commercial growers in some western states claim that they fear burglaries and robberies more than the police. If the marijuana laws did not exist, virtually all the crime and violence associated with its production and distribution would be eliminated.

Marijuana laws also deter many people from reporting unrelated crime. Users fear that, in their investigation, police will turn on the victims if there is a suspicion that the complainant is involved with marijuana.

The marijuana laws have eroded the confidence and trust that Americans have for the police. Our society, which began with freedom-loving patriots, has degenerated into a bloated bureaucracy of secret police who carry out surveillance against ordinary citizens. As long as marijuana remains illegal, police and citizens will only grow more suspicious of each other.

THE NEW PRISON BOOM

- The United States is now first in the world in its rate of incarceration in the first years of the 21st century, that rate has hovered at around 700 per 100,000 population.[17]
- The number of inmates in state and federal prisons has increased almost fivefold from 315,000 in 1980[18] to 1.4 million in 2001.[19] Adding the 630,000 inmates of local jails on any given day in 2001,[20] there were over 2 million persons

behind bars in the U.S. at the start of the 21st century. Drug offenses account for 57 percent of federal prison inmates[21] (up from 10 percent in 1983[22]), and just over 20 percent of state prisoners[23] and local jail inmates.[24]

- The number of persons on probation and parole has been growing dramatically, along with increases in the number of persons behind bars. There are now 6.6 million Americans incarcerated or on probation or parole, three and a half times the number in 1980.[25]

- Approximately 1 in 3 young black males ages 20 to 29 is under some type of correctional control, as is 1 in 15 young white males and 1 in 8 young Hispanic males.

- During the past 10 years state and federal governments planned $5.1 billion in new prison construction, at an average cost of $58,000 per medium-security cell. In the 1990s, 350 state correctional facilities were constructed, providing over 525,000 new beds to warehouse 81 percent more prisoners.[26]

MARIJUANA CRIME AND PUNISHMENT

- Over 10 million American citizens have been arrested for marijuana offenses since 1965.[27]

- In 2000, there were 734,500 marijuana arrests in the United States.[28]

- Of these arrests, about 88 percent (644,000) were for simple possession. The balance—often involving very small quantities—were for sale or cultivation.[29]

- Marijuana arrests made up approximately one-half of the total drug arrests for 2000.[30]

- From 1991 to 2000, the number of marijuana-possession

arrests tripled, while during that same period, according to the government's own figures, the number of 12- to 17-year-olds trying marijuana for the first time doubled.[31]

· Marijuana offenders made up approximately 20 percent of the federal prison population in 2000.[32] Drug offenders made up 57 percent of all federal prisoners in 2001, the largest prison population group by far.[33]

· At any one time there are estimated to be 59,300 people in jail for pot.[34] This number may be two to four times higher if people who have not been convicted, but are being detained while they wait for their cases to come up in court, are counted.

3

Economic Costs

Marijuana prohibition is costing taxpayers billions each year in enforcement costs. It is also costing us billions of dollars in missed opportunities: in taxes, profits, and wages.

In the 1960s, Humboldt County, California, was considered to be economically depressed. Its main industry, logging, had virtually closed down. Although the county officially attracted no new industries, by the early 1980s Humboldt appeared to be one of California's most prosperous areas. This was not completely reflected in the reported per capita income. Land values were also increasing astronomically. The reason? Humboldt County is in the heart of sinsemilla country, and the marijuana growers' spending was supporting the other businesses in the county. After the government crackdown on cultivation in the late 1980s, the county slipped back to its economically depressed state.

If marijuana were legalized, probably the first economic effect to be felt would be a significant drop in price, because of the elimination of the risk factor incidental to contraband substances.[1] This is what happened when alcohol prohibition was ended—the cost of liquor plummeted to about a third of its black-market cost. When other formerly contraband substances or procedures were reintroduced into the legal marketplace, their cost also fell substantially. For example, costs of abortions were reduced about 80 percent, and prices of formerly banned books were reduced about 30 percent.

The second effect would likely be greater availability of supply, and possibly a small increase in quantities consumed. Using a conservative 50 percent reduction in marijuana prices to the consumer and a relatively small increase in amount bought, the marijuana industry could gross $17 billion a year.

The third effect would be a new tax revenue stream for governments.[2] Based on experience with vice taxes on cigarettes, liquor, and other substances,[3] the federal excise and manufacturing taxes, licenses, and fees could generate about $7 billion a year in revenue for the government[4] including state licenses, taxes, and fees,[5] and these are just the direct revenues generated by regulation. Indirect revenues from taxes generated on sales of paraphernalia, from recreational establishments, and from new industries would increase the government's revenue stream considerably.[6]

Instead of this regular flow of revenue, the states and the federal government now "tax" the profits of the marijuana industry by seizing property and other assets used in the commission of illegal acts or purchased by virtue of the gains of them. Using law-enforcement agencies to collect taxes leaves those agencies wide open to possible corruption, not only from bribery but also from diversion of confiscated assets.[7]

There are about 1 million people employed in the commercial marijuana industry, including growers, retail dealers, wholesale distributors, and importers. Some of these are part-time or occasional. With sales at about $25 billion, we estimate net income for people involved in the U.S. marijuana industry at about $15 billion. This income is largely untaxed.

Marijuana lawyers, both prosecution and defense, are the people who probably profit most because of the marijuana laws. Prosecutors are ensured a steady stream of defendants and a high percentage of wins,[8] ensuring them high salaries and government benefits.

Even a simple possession bust is liable to cost the victim well over $7,500 in legal fees.[9] Cases in which the prosecution tries to prove wholesale distribution or conspiracy cost much more, ranging from $25,000 to "what it's worth to keep your hide out of jail."[10] Between 1 and 2 billion dollars is billed per year for legal fees in defense of marijuana cases.[11] For the most part, marijuana users have little experience with the judicial system, so they are often prey to incompetent attorneys who overcharge them or who do not represent them properly.

Domestic farmers supply a large percentage of the marijuana market; so much so that certain analysts estimate that marijuana is the largest domestic agricultural crop.[12] The estimated value of the U.S. marijuana crop is $15 billion to $20 billion a year; however, much of this is grown for personal rather than commercial use. That is more than 8 percent of the total gross revenue of legal agricultural crops ($240 billion in 2000).[13] As a percentage of net farm income, marijuana revenues are even higher. With estimated net profits of $15 billion, marijuana farming is 20 percent of total farm income ($46.4 billion in 2000).[14]

Of course, the huge majority of farmers do not grow marijuana, but perhaps more of them should look into it. While even large farms were being foreclosed at near record levels, marijuana farmers who grew a garden of less than 100 square feet earned $30,000-$50,000 a year.[15] "A few marijuana plants can double my income and increase my net several times," said a Wisconsin flower farmer.[16] It would seem that allowing farmers to grow marijuana would not only help save many small farms but also provide many new jobs, since marijuana farming and preparation are very labor intensive.

Even the cultivation of cannabis hemp—the nonpsychoactive variety of the plant—is outlawed in order to enforce the marijuana laws.[17] Hemp has many economic uses. It contains the longest fiber in the plant kingdom and is one of the strongest and most durable. It can be used for industrial and commercial applications, including insulation, textiles, clothing, and rope. The fiber and pulp can be used to manufacture nondeteriorating paper using a relatively pollution-free process.[18] The plant can also be used for biomass applications. Its seeds yield oil similar to linseed, which can be used in many commercial and industrial applications. After pressing the seed, the remaining mass becomes high-protein animal feed. In Eastern Europe and Central Asia, the seeds have been used for human consumption.

The U.S. is the only major industrialized nation that prohibits the cultivation of industrial hemp; at the same time, the U.S. is the number-one importer and consumer of hemp products.[19] Because American farm technology is generally superior to that of the rest of the world, legalizing marijuana and hemp cultivation would soon result in the United States becoming an exporter rather than an importer of the product. Instead of a net outflow of cash of some $10 billion to $15 billion a year (the amount we are spending on imported marijuana),[20] depending on the regulatory model used, estimates of potential hemp exports range from $60 million to $1 billion.[21]

In 1999, federal, state, and local governments spent over $7.7 billion enforcing marijuana laws,[22] money that might be better directed toward fighting violent crime and terrorism. Some of the government agencies with law-enforcement arms are the various federal and state police and customs services. Over twenty federal agencies are enlisted in the fight against marijuana use. These include the

FBI, CIA, DEA, Immigration and Naturalization, Navy, Air Force, Army, Customs, Post Office, Agriculture Department, U.S. Forestry Service, Department of Education, Department of Health and Welfare, Coast Guard, IRS, National Institute on Drug Abuse (NIDA), Commerce Department, Department of Transportation, National Institutes of Mental Health (NIMH), and the Treasury Department. Many of these are not included in the law-enforcement budget.

Costs of enforcement include funds spent for educational programs, arrests, incarceration, and judicial proceedings, but they do not include indirect costs, which include loss of income, potential welfare costs for dependents, and loss of productivity to society. According to the Shafer Commission's 1972 figures, over 82 percent of the individuals arrested for marijuana law violations had jobs or went to school, and fully 87 percent of them were permanent residents of their localities.[23] According to the National Household Survey on Drug Abuse (NHSDA), 2000, 77 percent of all drug users were employed.[24] Forty percent of marijuana arrestees do not make bail. On average, they are incarcerated for about forty-five days before trial, and lose thirty days of work due to the arrest.[25] Using the average salary of $35,300 a year,[26] the arrestee loses $4,073 in salary. Thus, the country loses $1,178,911,385 in total productivity.

Carl Hiassen, formerly a drug-crime reporter for the *Miami Herald,* said, "If you squeeze a balloon in one place it will pop out somewhere else. Pot's popularity will not go away. . . . I don't think it can be controlled. . . . It's no longer a law enforcement issue; it's an economic issue."[27]

According to a 1999 study by the Marijuana Policy Project (MPP), "At an average annual cost per prisoner per year of more than $20,000, the total cost to taxpayers of marijuana-related incarceration reaches more than $1.2 billion per year. (This does not include the cost of investigating, arresting, and prosecuting the hundreds of thousands of marijuana users arrested every year.)"[28] The cost to arrest, prosecute, and jail a single drug dealer can run as high as $450,000.

There is no doubt that the marijuana industry is here to stay and is part of this nation's economic life. This industry is unique in that it is subject to no government regulation regarding consumer protection, quality of product, distribution, imports, and taxation. If the industry remains illegal, it will continue to produce revenue and profits, but U.S. society will lose out on the economic benefits. The industry will persist as a costly expense to taxpayers, which pay for police, judicial, and penal expenses. Yet no tax revenue will be generated from this $25-billion-a-year industry, amounting to the biggest tax loophole ever given to any industry in the history of the United States. And the revenue losses from related but prohibited potential industries such as hemp cultivation are incalculable.

PUTTING AMERICA BEHIND BARS: THE COSTS MAY SURPRISE YOU

- Federal taxpayers spend far more per year to house one inmate ($23,000)[29] than to educate one child (approximately $8,000).[30]
- The Department of Justice budget grew over 800 percent between 1981–2002 compared to the Department of Education's budget, which grew only 285 percent.[31] The growth disparity is continuing.
- It costs more to send a person to prison for four years than it does to send a person to a university for four years.[32]
- "At the end of 2001 there were an estimated 1.2 million nonviolent offenders locked up in America at a cost of more than $24 billion annually."[33]

- "The total cost to taxpayers of marijuana-related incarceration reached more than \$1.2 billion per year. This does not include the cost of investigating, arresting, and prosecuting the hundreds of thousands of marijuana users arrested every year."[34]
- "The total number of drug prisoners represented 20.7 percent of the state and 62.6 percent of the federal inmate populations; however, the Bureau of Justice excluded unsentenced inmates and federal prisoners in state and private prisons, or state prisoners held in local jails or private facilities."[35]

HOW MANY PEOPLE USE MARIJUANA?

Our estimates of marijuana use were based on our assumption that conservatively, a third of the people who use marijuana answered truthfully on the U.S. Household Survey. However, we have no way of knowing whether these figures are accurate. Your guess may be as good as ours. If you think that 50 percent of the surveyed answered truthfully, then your use figures would be two-thirds of ours, totaling 20 million users. If you think that 20 percent answered truthfully, your estimates would be 40 percent higher than ours at 50 million.

Who knows? The honest answer is—nobody. It's hard to get information about illegal activities. And that's the honest answer.

Government studies estimate that there are approximately 10 million marijuana users in the U.S. who use approximately 1,000 metric tons (2,200 lbs.). This figure is based on the U.S Household Survey, in which a sampling of families are asked about their drug use. Even the government admits that these estimates may be low, because people are disinclined to report illegal behavior. We agree that the survey undercounts marijuana users; the question is by how much. The Drug Policy Report "What America's Users Spend on Illegal Drugs 1988–1998" says "it might be reasonable to inflate marijuana estimates by about one-third." We estimate that only between 25 and 33 percent of users answer this question factually. Below, we use the more conservative figure of one-third answering factually.

According to the government, the average user consumes 3.7 ounces of marijuana a year. We believe the figures to be much higher. We estimate there are 10 million people who use marijuana daily. They consume an average of half a gram daily, about 1/8 of an ounce per week. There are another 10 million who use regularly, 1 to 6 times weekly. Their average use comes to 1/8 of an ounce monthly. Another 10 million try marijuana once a month to once a year. They consume an average of 1/8 of an ounce per year.

10,000,000 people x 1/8 oz. x 52 weeks/year

= 65,000,000 oz./year

10,000,000 people x 1/8 oz. x 12 months/year

= 15,000,000 oz./year

10,000,000 people x 1/8 oz. x 1 year

= 1,250,000 oz./year

Total   **81,250,000 oz./year**

= 5,078,125 lbs./year

= 2,308 metric tons/year

Let's presume that half of the marijuana consumed is imported. About 65 percent of the imported marijuana comes from Mexico, 30 percent from Canada, and 5 percent from other countries, mostly in the Carribbean. Domestic sinsemilla either grown for personal use or commercially makes up the other 50 percent.

The tables below outline the value of the crop at retail.

Table 1: Retail Price per Metric Ton

1/8 ounce of U.S. dom $50 x 128[*]= $6,400/lb. x 2,200 lb.[**]
$$= \$14,080,000/\text{metric ton}$$

1/8 ounce of Mexican $12 x 128 = $1,536/lb. x 2,200 lb.
$$= \$3,379,200/\text{metric ton}$$

1/8 ounce of Canadian $35 x 128 = $4,480/lb. x 2,200 lb.
$$= \$9,856,000/\text{metric ton}$$

1/8 ounce of other $25 x 128   = $3,200/lb. x 2,200 lb.
$$= \$7,040,000/\text{metric ton}$$

[*] There are 128 eighth-ounces in 1 pound.
[**] There are approximately 2,200 pounds in 1 metric ton.

Table 2: Total Retail Value by Source

U.S. dom 50%= 1,254 metric tons @ $14,080,000 per ton
= $17,656,320,000
Mexico 32.5% = 750.1 metric tons @ $3,379,000 per ton
= $2,534,587,000
Canada 15% = 346.2 metric tons @ $9,856,000 per ton
= $3,412,147,000

Other 2.5%   = 57.7 metric tons @ $7,040,000 per ton
               = $4,062,080,000

Total Retail Value of Marijuana Used in U.S.: $27,665,134,000

We may be seriously underestimating marijuana use by a larger factor. If so, the retail value of marijuana consumed would be higher.

We assume that about 10 percent of the marijuana consumed is homegrown, produced for personal consumption. This material is not sold or bought. It removes the producer/consumer from the market. The result is that about 20 percent of the domestic sinsemilla is not marketed. This represents about:

250.8 metric tons @ $14,080,000 = $2,816,000,000

Our conservative figure for retail sales in the U.S. is $24,848,134,000.

Under a civil regulatory format, both the number of users and average use would rise slightly. The price would decline between one-third and two-thirds. If we figure a decline in price by 50 percent and include a slight rise in use, the approximate figure is $17 billion.

4

Health Effects

Never mind that the vast majority of Americans have expressed—in one public-opinion poll after another—little interest in trying these substances, even if they were legal, and never mind that most of those who have tried them have suffered few, if any, ill effects. The evidence of history and of science is drowned out by today's bogeymen. No rhetoric is too harsh, no penalty too severe.[1]

—Ethan Nadelmann

In terms of health effects, marijuana is easily defined: it is one of the most benign substances known to humans. This contrasts sharply with the picture of it painted by legalization opponents. For instance, Joyce Nalepka, founder and president of Parents for a Drug-Free Youth (which is now called "Drug-Free Kids" due to trademark problems) stated, "It is not a moral issue, it is a health issue."[2]

How can there be such divergent views? Simply put, the research cited by opponents has been done in vitro, or in laboratory experiments using situations that are abnormal. On the other hand, there is the recent body of evidence produced by the thirty-five-year "open laboratory," during which millions of people have been using marijuana in the U.S. and Western Europe. There are also the previous 2,000 years of documented observations to draw from.

Most government-sponsored research on marijuana is based on the "pathology theory," which tries to find problems caused by marijuana. This bias skews the results of the research because it forces researchers to start with preconceived notions. The researcher has a nonscientific interest in producing specific results. Researchers whose work has been rejected by scientific peers because it isn't replicable, such as Dr. Gabriel Nahas or the late Hardin Jones, were able to qualify for government grants. This continues today with funding for biased longitudinal studies and defunding of the Drug Abuse Warning Network (DAWN).

Government-paid researchers use spurious methods to conduct experiments. Researchers often use man-made cannabinoids, and extrapolate the experiments to natural marijuana, which contains a complex mixture of cannabinoids and THCs. The effects of natural marijuana are not actually studied.

In vitro experiments cannot measure the effect of a substance on the whole organism. Minor irritation to the respiratory tract can be tracked, but not the overall effect on the body or mind. In order to find out the true effects of marijuana on health, a program such as the Framingham Heart Study would have to be instituted. This would be an ongoing study of a population group over a number of years. The rates of illness and mortality would be measured periodically and compared with lifestyle. For the past thirty years, NIDA, the DEA, and other government agencies have been funding studies that focus on marijuana's negative effects, with little success. Given the government's interest in showing marijuana to be dangerous, any study that did show serious effects from marijuana use would have been well publicized. Ironically, some of the studies designed to find harm have shown that marijuana has positive effects. These studies have not been publicized.

Antimarijuana groups are quick to cite the statistics for treatment clinic admissions, stressing that the number of people seeking treatment for marijuana abuse has doubled since 1993. There were 220,000 admissions to treatment clinics for primary marijuana abuse in 1999.[3] However, a careful look at the people behind this statistic tells a different story.

Most of these "victims" turn out to be youths who were caught with marijuana and given a choice: jail or drug counseling.[4] In 1999, 57 percent of the persons in drug counseling because of their marijuana "problem" were referred by the criminal justice system, mostly as terms of probation or parole.[5] Only 16 percent were self-referrals,[6] and many of these faced legal proceedings and wanted to show the court "good faith" rehabilitation and remorse.

Marijuana admissions make up only 14 percent of all admissions for drug or alcohol treatment (1.6 million for alcohol and all drugs combined). The truly "voluntary" admissions—36,000 maximum of a total 223,600 total admissions of all ages in 1999—are a small fraction of the tens of millions of persons who regularly smoke marijuana. The 2000 NHSDA conservatively estimated that 1 in 20 people—that's around 11 million people—in the U.S. used marijuana in the past month.[7] All admissions are less than 2 percent of that number; voluntary admissions are less than a half of a percent. As few as 0.25 to 1 percent, or even fewer, consider marijuana a problem for which they need help. This is in marked contrast with heroin, for which 64 percent of users referred themselves to treatment and only 12 percent were referred by the criminal justice system.[8]

The number of people in treatment for a marijuana problem

increased consistently and substantially throughout the 1990s because of a sharp rise in arrests for marijuana. In 1993, 7 percent of all admissions to treatment were for marijuana; in 1999 the number had doubled to 14 percent. Likewise, in 1993, 55 of 100,000 persons age 12 and older were in a drug-treatment program for their primary marijuana problem; this rose each year and stood at 103 per 100,000 in 1999. Naturally, as marijuana treatment increasingly becomes a result of law enforcement, the proportion of criminal justice system referrals soars and the proportion of self-referrals subsides.

Most of the people who were admitted to programs for marijuana abuse used other drugs as well: In 1999, 57 percent of them used alcohol, and 8 percent used methamphetamines or amphetamines, 8 percent cocaine, 6 percent crack, 5 percent hallucinogens, and only 1 percent heroin.[9] The implication is that these are problem kids, and their drug abuse is partly a symptom of their condition.

Recent statistics were unavailable, but in 1981, a study found that for every month that a person attends a drug-abuse clinic for marijuana "abuse," there is a 1 percent chance he or she would switch to another, truly dangerous primary drug—alcohol, amphetamines, heroin, or PCP, for example.[10]

A thirty-seven-year-old San Francisco resident described his experiences as a court-ordered client of the Center for Special Problems, a drug-rehabilitation center in San Francisco. The sentence resulted from a conviction for possession of marijuana for sale:

There was a psychiatrist who drove down from Mann; he was part of a team. They held different kinds of classes. We were given a "therapeutic menu" in the morning, a kind of smorgasbord of activities from which we could choose, and we got credit for doing our own treatment. I had to go there up to three times a week for at least six months. The clients were from halfway houses: recovering alcoholics, speed freaks, PCP space cadets, as well as young people with psychological problems. The psychologist tried to get my life story down on paper. But mostly it was group therapy. They also had encounter sessions and Zen breathing exercises. Zen breathing is okay in a pastoral setting, but they had us sitting there doing deep breathing with the black exhaust from MUNI buses 10 feet away. In general, I tried not to remember my therapy sessions. They were just something I had to do. I filed it in that part of my mind that's inscribed with the zeros . . . so I could forget the whole thing.[11]

Nor do statistics on emergency cases bear out the opinion that marijuana is dangerous. Of the 96.2 million emergency-room visits in 2000, marijuana was mentioned in only 0.1 percent (or 1 out of every 1,000) of the cases.[12] This means that the patient admitted at some point in the medical interview to having used marijuana recently, usually within the preceding 24 hours. In 76 percent of these cases, marijuana was used in conjunction with another drug, such as alcohol or cocaine.[13]

DAWN counts a drug mention even when the reason for the emergency room visit is unrelated.[14] There were just over 96,000 mentions of marijuana.[15] In 38 percent of these incidences, the motive for seeking care was "psychic effects," as opposed to other drugs, where the reason most often cited was "dependence."[16] If approximately 30 million people use marijuana at least once per year, then 32 in every 10,000 users reported their marijuana use during an emergency-room

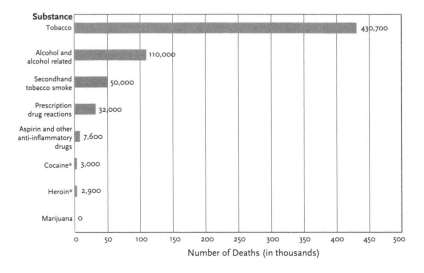

* Alone and in combination with other substances

U.S. Drug-related Deaths in the U.S. Although many try to demonize marijuana or stress its dangers, the fact remains that marijuana is one of the safest medicines known to humans. Still, marijuana remains a Schedule I drug, the most restrictive category possible. Source: This data is derived from the sources indicated in chapter 4 endnotes 20–27.

visit, and only 9 in every 10,000 marijuana users visited the emergency-room specifically for the psychic effects, or getting too high.

No evidence exists that anyone has ever died of a marijuana overdose.[17] Tests performed on mice have shown that the ratio of cannabinoids (the chemicals in marijuana that make you stoned) necessary for overdose to the amount necessary for intoxication is 40,000 to 1;[19] that ratio for alcohol is between 4 and 10 to 1.[20] By contrast, alcohol kills nearly 20,000 Americans every year, and alcohol-related injuries and diseases kill 90,000 more.[20]

Actually, marijuana law enforcement is more of a threat to the health of marijuana users than the herb itself. Every year, marijuana users die or are killed by police officers as the direct result of the enforcement of marijuana laws.

Think about this for just a moment. People die because our government is trying to "protect" us from the "dangers" of marijuana, a natural herb that has never caused a death. Up to 30 million people risk this kind of governmental "protection" when they use cannabis.

DRUG DEATHS IN THE UNITED STATES IN A TYPICAL YEAR

- Tobacco kills about 430,700.[21]
- Alcohol and alcohol-related diseases and injuries kill about 110,000.[22]
- Secondhand tobacco smoke kills about 50,000.[23]
- Aspirin and other anti-inflammatory drugs kill 7,600.[24]
- Cocaine kills about 500 alone, and another 2,500 in combination with another drug.[25]
- Heroin kills about 400 alone, and 2,500 more in combination with another drug.[26]
- Adverse reactions to prescription drugs total 32,000.[27]
- Marijuana kills 0.[28]

In 1999, 18,443 people died from licit and illicit drug use, about 3.5 percent of the number killed by alcohol and tobacco.[29]

MARIJUANA AND DRIVING

Here's what the National Highway Transportation Safety Administration (NHTSA) has to say about a 1996 study of marijuana's effect on actual driving performance conducted on freeways and urban roads in the Netherlands with various dosages of marijuana:[30]

- Marijuana intoxication in drivers is "in no way unusual compared to many medicinal drugs."
- Marijuana does have some effect on driving ability but is "not profoundly impairing."
- Unlike alcohol, which encourages risky driving, marijuana appears to produce greater caution, apparently because the users are more aware of their mental state and able to compensate for it.

More recent studies verify these findings. The National Organization for the Reform of Marijuana Laws (NORML) Foundation has summarized a large body of research about marijuana's effect on driving performance. These included driving-simulator studies, on-road performance studies, crash-culpability studies, and summary reviews of existing evidence. NORML concluded, "To date, the result of this research is fairly consistent: Marijuana has a measurable yet relatively mild effect on psychomotor skills, yet it does not appear to play a significant role in vehicle crashes, particularly when compared to alcohol."[31]

5

Hemp: Industrial Applications

Make the most of the hemp seed. Sow it everywhere.

—George Washington

Hemp. It's marijuana's nonpsychoactive sister. You couldn't get a buzz if you smoked a bale of hemp, but it's still illegal to grow it in the United States.

Industrial hemp is legally grown in more than thirty countries.[1] For thousands of years, people grew hemp and prospered. It flourishes without pesticides, and birds happily devour their favorite seed.[2] Thomas Jefferson considered hemp so vital to America that he risked his life to smuggle hemp seeds out of France. George Washington grew hemp and instructed his caretaker at Mt. Vernon: "Make the most of the hemp seed. Sow it everywhere."

Too bad we've failed to heed Washington's wisdom. Using modern processing techniques, hemp can be used in place of petrochemicals. Instead of synthetic plastics made from oil, we can use natural fiber and processed bioplastic derivatives.

Plastics and polyester rely on foreign oil, while cotton consumes enormous amounts of water, fertilizer, herbicides, and pesticides.[3]

Half the trees cut down each year are used for paper. Whole old-growth forests are still being leveled for pulp. Hemp, which takes a single growing season to reach maturity, could be used instead.

In the 1930s, an unholy alliance of forest magnates, ex-Prohibition agents, and chemical and industrial pharmaceutical companies used the public's fear of drugs and concern for kids to end the use of not only marijuana, but also industrial hemp.

The marijuana laws were used to replace natural hemp products and pharmaceuticals with high-profit synthetic substitutes. Ironically, the prohibition against marijuana and hemp helped create a far more deadly society-wide addiction to petroleum and plastics. Our chronic use of petrochemicals is degrading our environment. It has become so toxic that we are witnessing the largest extinction of species since the demise of the dinosaurs.

On June 1, 1996, hemp activist and noted Hollywood actor Woody Harrelson was arrested and charged with cultivation of fewer than five marijuana plants after he brazenly planted four seeds of industrial hemp in full view of Lee County Sheriff William Kilburn in Lexington, Kentucky.

Why would a pampered movie star want to get himself arrested? Here's what Woody had to say about his courageous act of civil disobedience:

Industrial hemp, like the four certified seeds I planted, was first grown in Kentucky 250 years ago. It is currently grown in other countries across the globe, including France, England, Canada, Australia, China, Hungary, and the Ukraine. Industrial hemp has little THC, the psychoactive ingredient in marijuana. It cannot be used as a drug. None of the countries that allow industrial hemp production have experienced any problems relating to the crop.

Industrial hemp is very clean and easy to grow. It is one of the most environmentally sound sources of industrial fiber in the world. Environmentally friendly detergents, plastics, paints, varnishes, cosmetics, and textiles are already being made from it in Europe. . . . Industrial hemp can meet our fiber needs while also revitalizing our struggling rural economies.

Congress never intended to make legitimate industrial hemp farming the same as marijuana cultivation. I planted industrial hemp and got arrested because someone must highlight this difference, and in order to truly know the law, one must test the law. I think it is time for all of us to make a stand . . . for environmentally friendly rural economic development. If the people lead, the leaders will follow.[4]

Woody planted four seeds. Had he planted a fifth seed, he would have been charged with a felony. Some of our greatest Americans, like Jefferson and Washington, who grew hemp and praised its uses, would be felons today.

Why should industrial hemp be legal? Here are just a few reasons:

- Hemp requires no herbicides or pesticides and needs much less water than cotton. It is an extremely vigorous annual and high yielder, producing up to five tons of usable material per acre.
- Hemp seed oil is a nonpolluting drying oil that can be used for paints and varnishes. Some of the world's greatest oil paintings were done with hemp-based paints.

- Hemp oil is valuable as a lubricant.
- New research shows that hemp oil is also a premier oil for human consumption. It is a source of essential fatty acids, which are missing in most other oils.[5]
- Hemp is already being used in place of trees for pressboard, particleboard, and core concrete construction molds.
- Paper made from hemp is acid-free. It is stronger and lasts far longer than paper made from trees.
- Hemp fabrics are far stronger and more resistant to mold than any other natural fiber.
- Builders in France and Germany use hemp for construction material, replacing drywall and plywood.
- Hemp can be used to manufacture plastic plumbing pipe, replacing such toxic materials as polyvinyl chloride (PVC).
- Hemp fiber is already being used in place of glass fiber in surfboards and snowboards. Hemp could also provide the resin itself.

In 1991, the U.S. hemp industry grossed about $5 million. Over the last decade, imports of hemp products have increased exponentially. In 1999, more than 1.5 million pounds of raw hemp fiber were imported. In 2002, the U.S. was expected to import $500 million of hemp and hemp products, according to Bob Newland, Libertarian Party candidate for attorney general and supporter of the Industrial Hemp Act.[6]

For ideological reasons, the federal government refuses to allow farmers to grow hemp, despite the fact that industrial hemp is currently grown legally throughout much of Europe, Asia, and Canada. The European Union even offers subsidies to hemp growers. More than ten states have passed resolutions or legislation authorizing industrial hemp "trial crops."[7] Hawaii leads the pack in legislation and has grown its first crop under the direction of Dr. Dave West.[8]

Erwin "Bud" Sholts, director of the Wisconsin Agriculture Department's marketing division, said, "[Hemp] is the most value-added, prolific fiber crop man can grow." Sholts acknowledged that hemp is an emotional issue, but points out that "other nations with drug laws as tough or tougher than ours have overcome this hurdle."[9]

Despite the support that hemp has within the farm community, USDA agents have been advised to steer clear of hemp to avoid opposition from Congress or the administration. USDA staff was discouraged from involvement in, or even acknowledgment of, industrial hemp.[10] The Bush administration took anti-hemp policy to a new extreme, attempting unsuccessfully to ban hemp foods and cosmetics. In 2002, Canadian company Kenex Ltd. filed a $20 million arbitration claim against the U.S. federal government for losses as a result of the short-lived ban, which infringed on the North American Free Trade Agreement (NAFTA).[11]

Clearly no progress can be made toward restoring hemp as a cash crop until the government backs away from its irrational fear of hemp. Many hemp advocates hope to make a case for distinguishing "rope" from "dope." However, the DEA refuses to make any such distinction. As one officer said, "Even 1 percent dope is still dope." As long as marijuana remains illegal, self-serving DEA bureaucrats will continue to insist that hemp remain illegal as well.

6

Medical Applications

Nearly all medicines have toxic, potentially lethal effects. But marijuana is not such a substance. There is no record in the extensive medical literature describing a proven, documented cannabis-induced fatality. . . . Marijuana, in its natural form, is one of the safest therapeutically active substances known to man.[1]

—DEA Administrative Law Judge Francis L. Young

Of all the reasons to legalize marijuana, none is more compelling than its medical usage. Marijuana has a wide variety of therapeutic applications, and is frequently beneficial in treating the following conditions:

- **AIDS.** Marijuana reduces the nausea, vomiting, and loss of appetite caused by both the ailment itself and as a side effect of treatment with AZT and other medicines.[2]
- **Asthma.** Several studies have shown that THC acts as a bronchodilator and reverses bronchial constriction. Although conventional bronchodilators work faster than marijuana,

THC has been shown to last longer and with considerably less risk.[3]

- **Arthritis and Other Autoimmune Diseases.** In addition to its effectiveness in controlling the pain associated with arthritis, new evidence shows that marijuana is an autoimmune modulator.[4]

- **Cancer.** Marijuana stimulates the appetite and alleviates nausea and vomiting, common side effects of chemotherapy treatment. People undergoing chemotherapy find that smoking marijuana is an antinauseant often more effective than mainstream medications.[5]

- **Chronic Pain.** Marijuana alleviates the debilitating, chronic pain caused by myriad disorders and injuries.[6]

- **Depression and Other Mood Disorders.** Marijuana has been shown to help dysphoria gently and naturally.[7] Conventional antidepressant and mood-stabilizing drugs like selective serotonin reuptake inhibitors (e.g., Prozac, Zoloft, etc.), lithium, tricyclics, and MAO inhibitors have serious health risks and side effects.

- **Epilepsy.** Marijuana is used as an adjunctive medicine to prevent epileptic seizures. Some patients find that they can reduce dosage of other seizure-control medications while using cannabis.[8]

- **Glaucoma.** Marijuana can reduce intraocular pressure, alleviating pain and slowing (and sometimes stopping) the progress of the condition.[9]

- **Menstrual Cramps and Labor Pain.** Many women use pot to ease the pain of menstrual cramps and childbirth, but don't disclose their behavior for fear their babies will be taken away from them. Women who use marijuana for labor and delivery report that it is far more effective pain relief than conventional drugs, and that their babies are more alert at birth.[10] One study of such marijuana babies showed that children of moderate smokers show superior psychomotor skills.[11]

- **Multiple Sclerosis.** Marijuana limits the muscle pain and spasticity caused by the disease, and relieves tremor and unsteady gait.[12] (Multiple sclerosis is the leading cause of neurological disability among young and middle-aged adults in the United States, and strikes two to three times more women than men.[13])

- **Muscle Spasm and Spasticity.** Medical marijuana has been clinically shown to be effective in relieving these.[14]

- **Migraine Headaches.** Marijuana not only relieves pain, but also inhibits the release of serotonin during attacks. [15]

- **Paraplegia and Quadriplegia.** Many paraplegics and quadriplegics have discovered that cannabis not only relieves their pain more safely than opiates, but also suppresses their muscle twitches and tremors.[16]

- **Pruritis (Itching).** Marijuana can be used orally and topically for this condition and may be more effective than corticosteroids and antihistamines.[17]

- **Insomnia.** Research shows pot can help people sleep—without the side effects or tolerance problems of other hypnotics. Cannabidiol is the active ingredient in pot that induces sleep.[18]

In 1988, Judge Francis Young of the DEA found marijuana to be "the safest therapeutic substance known to man" and urged its reclassification and distribution for medical uses. Jon Gettman, NORML director from 1986 to 1989, filed a petition to reschedule marijuana in 1995. Gettman contended that marijuana should be rescheduled from a

DEA Federal Drug Scheduling Guidelines

	Schedule I	Schedule II
SUBSTANCES	Marijuana, PCP, LSD, Heroin, Quaaludes	Amphetamines, Cocaine, Codeine, Morphine, Methadone, Opium
POTENTIAL FOR ABUSE	High potential for abuse	High potential for abuse
MEDICAL USE	No currently accepted medical use in treatment in the U.S.	Medical use in treatment currently accepted in the U.S., possibly with severe restrictions
LIKELIHOOD OF DEPENDENCE	There is no safe acceptable use even under medical supervision	Abuse may lead to severe psychological or physical dependence

Sources: "Federal Laws Concerning Drugs," Integrated Publishing, Spring, TX (http://www.tpub.com/maa/65.htm) and DEA Briefs and Background, Drug Policy, Drug Scheduling (http://www.usdoj.gov/dea/pubs/scheduling.html)

Schedule III	Schedule IV	Schedule V
Marinol, Anabolic Steroids, Barbiturates, Phenobarbital	Xanax, Valium, Halcion, Ambien	Robitussin A-C, Lomotil
Moderate potential for abuse (lower potential than substances in Schedules I or II)	Low potential for abuse (lower potential than substances in Schedule III)	Lowest potential for abuse (lower potential than substances in Schedule IV)
Medical use in treatment currently accepted in the U.S.	Medical use in treatment currently accepted in the U.S.	Medical use in treatment currently accepted in the U.S.
Abuse may lead to moderate or low physical dependence or high psychological dependence	Abuse may lead to limited physical dependence or psychological dependence	Abuse may lead to limited physical dependence or psychological dependence

Schedule I to a Schedule II drug, since it fails to meet the legal criteria for Schedule I classification, which is the most restrictive category under the Controlled Substances Act.[19] Both Schedule I and Schedule II drugs are substances with "a high potential for abuse." The difference is that Schedule I drugs "have no currently accepted medical application in the U.S.," while Schedule II drugs, such as morphine, cocaine, and PCP, can be prescribed for a currently accepted medical use.[20] The Federal Drug Administration (FDA) advised against a reclassification in 2001. On May 24, 2002, the United States Court of Appeals for the District of Columbia ruled to uphold the DEA's determination, maintaining marijuana's Schedule I status.

In 1999, the Institute of Medicine, a branch of the National Academy of Sciences (NAS), issued a report titled *Marijuana and Medicine: Assessing the Science Base*.[21] Among the findings of this committee of medical experts: "The accumulated data indicate a potential therapeutic value for cannabinoid drugs, particularly for symptoms such as pain relief, control of nausea and vomiting, and appetite stimulation." While they were cautionary about smoked marijuana as medicine, they acknowledged that people suffering from some chronic conditions have no clear alternative to smoked marijuana for pain relief.[22] These judicial findings have been totally ignored by the DEA and other federal agencies.

After years of suppression by the government, the truth about medical marijuana is finally coming out. Dr. Tod Mikuriya, former director of marijuana research for the entire federal government, explains: "I was hired by the government to provide scientific evidence that marijuana was harmful. As I studied the subject, I began to realize that marijuana was once widely used as a safe and effective medicine. But the government had a different agenda, and I had to resign."[23]

From 1994 until 1996, Mikuriya spent much of his time studying patients who were receiving medical marijuana under the auspices of the San Francisco Cannabis Buyers' Club. (In July 1996, the club was closed by court order at the instigation of California Attorney General Dan Lundgren.) Mikuriya has continued his work with patients since then. Eventually the dispensary reopened, only to be closed again by the federal government in 2000. He is currently medical coordinator of the California Cannabis Centers and a member of the city of Oakland's Medical Marijuana Work Group.

In February 1994, Dennis Peron and friends founded the Buyers' Club and began openly selling cannabis to people with HIV, cancer, intractable pain, and multiple sclerosis. Their daring actions, which they called "compassionate use," were serious violations of federal law, but Peron and his group were determined to provide sick people with an herb that could help them gain weight and cope with pain. Fortunately, the city of San Francisco was squarely on their side.

Medical authorities such as Dr. DuPont of NIMH have claimed that marijuana will never be accepted as a medicine because dosages can't be controlled.[24] This is not necessarily the case, for patients report that they control dosages when they smoke. One patient summarized a prevailing opinion among his peers: "Doctors hate the idea of patients self-medicating . . . but we patients know our bodies, and we can do a better job than doctors at judging when we've reached an effective dosage."[25]

It is true that smoked marijuana is very fast acting, so it is easy for an experienced patient to regulate his or her dose. In addition, more patients are using tinctures, foods, and pills to standardize dosage.

DuPont also insists that regular marijuana is dangerous, and that patients should receive their treatments in the form of capsulized Marinol. Generically known as dronabinol, Marinol is a highly concentrated synthetic formulation of delta-9-THC, one of the active forms of THC found in natural marijuana.[26]

Dr. Mikuriya strongly disagrees. "There are over twenty active forms of THC and over sixty different cannabinoids which are active in marijuana. Marinol contains only one form of THC and no other cannabinoids, so it's just part of the answer."[27] It's an expensive prescription drug, at $10 or more per capsule. When used as recommended, it costs $80 a day, or up to $1,000 a week. In comparison, natural marijuana can be grown inexpensively.

So far, nine states and the District of Columbia have recognized this and legalized growing and/or possession of marijuana by patients or their caregivers; however, federal laws continue to make growing under any circumstance a crime.

Marinol has two other major shortcomings:

- Because it contains pure THC, it packs a powerful wallop that many patients find unpleasant and even incapacitating. Natural marijuana contains many other nonpsychoactive ingredients with medical actions of their own that can counteract the adverse effect of THC.[28]
- In patients suffering from nausea, swallowing capsules may itself provoke vomiting. In 2002, Dr. Notcutt reported results of human testing for pain relief in MS patients. Neither THC nor CBD was effective alone as an analgesic. However, when combined, they were extremely efficacious.[29]

Many patients and physicians avoid Marinol because they have found that smoking natural marijuana delivers THC more efficiently and allows them to continue their normal activities. Dennis Peron is even more adamant: "Marinol costs up to $35,000 a year and doesn't work. Our patients at the Buyers' Club who have tried it say it made them so stoned they couldn't function or that it had other adverse effects. Also, Marinol is a pill, so you have to keep it down long enough to help the nausea. That's nuts, and it doesn't work."[30]

The continuing prohibition of medical marijuana is based more on political than scientific considerations. Although during the 1970s the government supported exploration into marijuana's therapeutic potential, it has now taken on the role of blocking new research and opposing any change in marijuana's legal status.[31] Agencies such as NIMH have steadfastly refused to allow investigations into the benefits of marijuana.[32]

More than twenty states have passed legislation to allow marijuana's use as a medicine, but federal law preempts these statutes.[33] Although the feds insist that marijuana has no medical benefits, there is ample evidence that medical marijuana works:

- Forty-four percent of oncologists responding to a questionnaire said they had recommended marijuana to their cancer patients. Fifty-four percent said they would recommend medical marijuana if it were legal.[34]
- Several studies have clearly shown that marijuana is effective in reducing nausea and vomiting.[35]
- Patients undergoing cancer chemotherapy have found smoking marijuana to be more effective than available pharmaceutical medications, including Marinol.[36]
- Marijuana is also smoked by thousands of AIDS patients to treat the symptoms associated with both the disease and drug therapy. Because it stimulates appetite, marijuana also counters HIV-related "wasting," allowing AIDS patients to gain weight and prolong their lives.[37]

Because of prohibition, millions of people are suffering needless pain, wasting away because they are unable to eat, or struggling to live while doped up on dangerous, addictive synthetic drugs. Marijuana decriminalization can give these unfortunate people a natural, inexpensive herb to relieve their pain, while restoring their appetite and their enjoyment of life.

While activists and patients battle with the government over medical marijuana, an even bigger health issue may be at stake. Scientists have discovered that hemp oil, the nonpsychoactive oil from marijuana seeds, may hold the key to fighting cancer, AIDS, and other common diseases.

Andrew Weil, a Harvard-trained doctor, regularly prescribes hemp oil for his patients. Here's why:

> It has a remarkable fatty acid profile, being high in the desirable omega-3s and also delivering some GLA (gamma-linolenic acid) that is absent from the fats we normally eat. Nutritionally oriented doctors believe all of these compounds to be beneficial to health. Hemp oil contains 57 percent linoleic (LA) and 19 percent linolenic (LNA) acids, in the three-to-one ratio that matches our nutritional needs. These are the essential fatty acids (EFAs)—so called because the body cannot make them and must get them from external sources.[38]

Weil reports his patients show marked improvement after using hemp oil, noting that their general health and energy improve, as does their appearance. Weil is also impressed by hemp oil's ability to improve the health and appearance of hair.[39]

How could oil from marijuana seeds be so effective? In his book

Fats that Heal, Fats that Kill, Udo Erasmus says "hemp seed oil appears to be one of nature's most perfectly balanced EFA oils. It contains both EFAs in the right proportions for long-term use, and also contains gamma-linolenic acid (GLA). It is the only vegetable oil with this combination."[40]

Erasmus shows how EFAs transport oxygen and confer immunity to cells constructed of these rare but essential fatty acids. "EFAs are extremely important for health and vitality. EFA deficiencies are correlated with degenerative diseases such as cardiovascular disease, cancer, diabetes, multiple sclerosis, skin afflictions, dry skin, premenstrual syndrome, behavioral problems, poor wound healing, arthritis, glandular atrophy, weakened immune functions, and sterility (especially males)."[41] Erasmus has made a thorough study of all forms of EFA-containing oils and concludes, "GLA has been shown to help the metabolism of fats and prevent fat deposits. Hemp oil is the only common seed oil that contains GLA."[42] Erasmus points out that GLA also serves as a precursor to prostaglandins, short-lived chemicals that have hormone-like effects on virtually every aspect of our health.[43]

The only downside to hemp oil is that the molecule is fragile and breaks down quickly when exposed to light, heat, or air. Hemp seed, from which the oil is extracted, may be legally possessed in the United States only if it has been heated or fumigated to make it sterile. Heating damages the seed oils, and fumigation can add toxins.

Although there is persuasive evidence that hemp oil has incredible health benefits, our government allows only sterile, imported hemp seeds, so hemp oil costs four to five times more than other oils. As with medical marijuana, this opposition to hemp oil comes from self-serving bureaucratic policies and cultural prejudice. No matter what the research shows, the DEA and other federal agencies are determined to oppose any use of marijuana or hemp.

Marijuana prohibition has caused us to pay a terrible price in pain and suffering, especially for those who are critically ill and might otherwise benefit from this unique herbal medicine. The drug warriors assure us that "marijuana has no medical uses," but the truth is that as long as marijuana is illegal, all of us are being denied a valuable medicine which can provide nontoxic, long-lasting relief, and even cures for a host of common ailments.

7

National Security

The DEA estimates that half of the marijuana consumed in the United States is imported.[1] It is distributed in virtually every county in the United States. Most of this product originates in Mexico.[2] In fact, the economy of some regions of Mexico would collapse without the marijuana industry. Recently, Canada has been listed in government reports as a source country for high-grade imported sinsemilla.[3]

Imported marijuana is typically unprocessed—it enters the United States in the form of raw, dried vegetable matter. Because of the surreptitious means of entry into the country, it is also uninspected. There has not yet been any news of contamination of domestic vegetation from blights or bugs arriving in the marijuana, but the distribution of uninspected material places commercial agriculture in a precarious position. Coming as it is from areas that remain largely unresearched as to agricultural pests and diseases, the threat to the domestic food supply is apparent. If just one pest or disease enters the food chain, it could seriously damage whole sectors of our agricultural community. California and Florida's experience with the Mediterranean fruit fly and the introduction into the United States of the Japanese beetle and the gypsy moth are but a sampling of imported insects that have created serious problems for farmers and gardeners alike.

The way Mexican marijuana is handled before it is shipped here creates opportunities for spoilage and disease. The marijuana is harvested and then dried in the open. Coca-Cola or another binding agent is poured over the dried pot, and the mass is pressed into bricks. Weeks may pass before these bricks of marijuana are brought over the border, allowing plenty of time for mold and bacteria to grow. In fact, the Centers for Disease Control has reported several epidemic-proportion outbreaks of illness resulting from contaminated or improperly handled marijuana. In one case in 1981, the marijuana was contaminated with animal feces and bacteria. As a result, eighty-five people were hospitalized for salmonella in Georgia, Alabama, California, Arizona, Massachusetts, Ohio, and Michigan.[4] In another case, smokers developed lung problems after smoking improperly handled marijuana; the material had become moldy during shipment. Other infectious agents have been *Aspergillus* and *Penicillium* species of molds, and *Streptococcus* and *Candida* species of bacteria.[5]

Despite increasing government efforts to stem the flow of imports through criminal sanctions, a significant number of importers are successful. As long as some uninspected marijuana is imported, the threat remains. The only way to be certain that no uninspected marijuana enters the country is to regulate the commerce so that physical inspections can be made at ports of entry.

Domestically grown marijuana is subject to the same health hazards, and some of the domestic crop would not be able to pass an Agriculture Department inspection either. Domestic marijuana may be contaminated with insect eggs or mold, and domestic diseases and pests often pose greater threats than foreign ones because they are much better suited for survival in their home environment.

Consumers of this uninspected material run the risks of ingesting these germs and impurities, as well as other toxins. Infected marijuana is more likely to be sold in commercial markets than in the medical-marijuana dispensaries. In personal communications with several medical-cannabis dispensary directors, I was told that they use a photographer's loupe to detect mites, insects, and other contaminants such as fur or molds. They can smell some bacterial infections from the acrid odor that they produce. They invariably reject this produce.

Herbicides and pesticides that have been banned in the United States because of their deleterious effects on human health are still used in Mexico. Since marijuana plants are often grown in wild areas and would be vigorously attacked by exotic bugs unless large amounts of chemicals are applied, the plants are often contaminated with high levels of herbicides and pesticides. U.S. growers sometimes use pesticides approved for ornamental plants, not ingestibles. Pesticide residues are likely to be found on both domestic and imported material.

Paraquat, Round-Up^{TM}, and other herbicides are far more dangerous than marijuana. By promoting the use of herbicides to battle marijuana growers, our government is placing citizens at greater risk than if it let them smoke marijuana.

Marijuana smuggled from Mexico comes to the United States mostly by truck.[6] At the southwest border of the U.S., 747 metric tons were seized in 1998.[7] The seizure of this cannabis required tens of thousands of worker-hours. This costly vigil diverts equipment and funds, that could be used in other pursuits that would better serve the American people.

Even with military surveillance, marijuana continues to get through. Researchers have pointed out that there is no shortage of

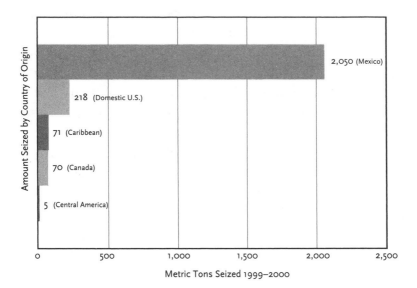

Where in the World Is U.S. Marijuana Coming From? Marijuana Seizures 1999–2000. Marijuana-seizure records support common sense: most U.S. pot originates on the North American continent. The overwhelming majority of U.S. cannabis is either grown domestically or imported from Mexico and, to a lesser degree, from Canada. Our neighbors in the Caribbean and Central America account for the rest. Contrary to the new propaganda campaign linking drugs and terrorism, the countries in this chart are not on the suspect list. Source: United Nations Office for Drug Control and Crime Prevention (ODCCP) Studies on Drugs and Crime, *Global Illicit Drug Trends 2002*, p. 129.

supply in the global market because price has steadily gone down, while purity has gone up—an indication that supply is meeting demand.[8] In the 1980s, the government estimated that it seized between 10 and 15 percent of all smuggled marijuana, but it no longer gives estimates of what percentage it seizes. The number of trucks and the manner of concealing the shipments has grown far beyond the capacity of customs and border-control agents. The seizure of so much cannabis indicates a problem with border control. Smugglers would not attempt to import cannabis if there were a high chance of seizure, since it would not have an attractive risk-reward ratio.

Marijuana prohibition affects U.S. relations with other countries. American actions toward trading partners are often driven by anti-marijuana policies. Operation Intercept was a program developed by the Nixon administration in 1969 to stem the flow of marijuana imports from Mexico. The program included thorough, time-consuming vehicle checks at the Mexico-U.S. border. This slowed the traffic across the border to a snail's pace. Some observers conjecture that the real purpose of Operation Intercept was not to find marijuana smugglers, but to force Mexico to change its marijuana policy. The Mexican government quickly saw the economic implications of Operation Intercept: if Mexico did not agree to help the United States dry up the flow of marijuana into this country, the U.S. government would stifle economic activity on the border. The operation lasted only a few weeks, but it was enough to get Mexico to agree to spray paraquat on marijuana fields.[9]

Other countries have also felt the lash of American marijuana policy. The Jamaican, Thai, and Colombian governments have all been subject to American carrot-and-stick demands. In each of these countries, the American government has interfered in internal politics, threatening to destabilize governments whose marijuana policies conflict with those of the United States. The U.S.'s "Plan Colombia," instituted in 1999 and enlarged by President G. W. Bush, is destined to create havoc in that part of South America. Now that Canada is legalizing cannabis, U.S. Drug Czar Walters is threatening to disrupt trade with our northern neighbor.[10]

Since the United States is a prohibition country, production of the herb becomes a black-market process in countries that import to us. This sets up officials of foreign governments—even those who are supposedly cooperating with the U.S. government—to be corrupted by marijuana commerce, giving international crime syndicates incentives to circumvent the laws and international law-enforcement agencies.

Some officials of foreign countries allow the illegal trade to flourish in order to placate their rural citizens, who depend on the crop for their livelihood. Thus, although there may be no direct payments from growers to government officials, safeguarding the growers may be a self-preservation tactic for elected representatives.

Other economic aspects of the illegal trade make it a corrupting influence. Marijuana commerce plays a significant role in the balance of trade of exporting countries. The federal government seized 329 metric tons of Mexican marijuana or marijuana transported through Mexico in 2000.[11] The value of the cannabis seized at the Mexican border ranged between $400 and $1,000 per pound.[12] At $700 a pound, the 796,400 pounds seized had a value of $557,480,000. However, this represents only a small portion of the estimated 7,500 tons imported to the U.S. from Mexico (see p. 25 in chapter 3 on economics). The bill for these imports came to $11.55 billion. It provided Mexicans with income that they otherwise could never have had, and provided the nation with American dollars necessary to pay for items it imported. In 2001, Mexico's legal exports to the U.S. were $131 billion.[13] Marijuana accounted for almost 9 percent of Mexico's imports to the U.S. The trade is ingrained in the social, economic, and political systems of both countries. If it is stopped, there will be economic dislocation. If it flourishes, there are political and criminal consequences.

The U.S. government was active in cannabis eradication in Jamaica through the 1970s and 1980s, providing millions of dollars for counternarcotics assistance.[14] It de-escalated efforts throughout the 1990s. In 2001, Jamaica's National Commission on Ganja recommended that marijuana use and possession be decriminalized. The commission reported that "The prosecution of simple possession for personal use itself diverts the justice system from what ought to be a primary goal, namely the suppression of the criminal trafficking in substances, such as crack cocaine, that are ravaging urban and rural communities with addiction and corrupting otherwise productive people."[15] They added that prosecuting people for simple possession of cannabis discredits the legitimacy of the Jamaican legal system in the eyes of the general populace.[16] Commission researchers found that almost one-third of Jamaican adults smoke marijuana on a regular basis. The recommended change in law would make the possession of personal amounts legal.[17] The current laws punish possession of a small quantity of marijuana with either a fine or up to ten days in jail.[18]

After the commission announced their recommendation, the U.S. was quick to issue threats. Orna Bloom, a spokesperson for the U.S. Embassy in Jamaica, said that the U.S. opposed the liberalization of Jamaica's cannabis laws because "it creates the perception . . . that marijuana is not harmful."[19] Michael Koplovsky, another U.S. embassy spokesperson, simply stated U.S. opposition to marijuana's decriminalization, immediately invoking the 1988 UN Drug Convention, of which Jamaica is a signator.[20] He implied that Jamaica would not receive its annually renewable stamp of approval, which would cause the country to lose most of its foreign assistance from the U.S. and the World Bank.[21] Dr. Dennis Forsythe, a sociologist and advocate for policy change in Jamaica, remarked to the Jamaican newspaper *The Gleaner,* "This is a domestic affair. It is a recommendation for self-help, not to export ganja, so we are not imposing it on anybody. . . . The Commission's recommendation is in keeping with the sentiments of the Jamaican people. If America is so much for democracy then to deny us certification because of this is in flagrant breach of such principles."[22]

The international policing organizations pose a major threat to democracy. Using marijuana as a pretext, they have the power to cross international borders with impunity, to accomplish "international policing." Some of them function under the auspices of the United Nations: for example, the International Association of Chiefs of Police (IACOP) and the Subcommittee of Illicit Drug Traffic and Related Matters. Other voluntary organizations and governmental agencies, such as various nations' narcotic law-enforcement agencies, function outside the UN framework.

The leaders of these organizations constantly seek more police powers in their struggle against the marijuana trade. But because they operate outside the limits of the national laws of the various states, they are an especially serious threat. Many of these agencies consider themselves above local law and thereby threaten the very democracies that they are supposed to uphold.

The marijuana laws pose a number of serious threats to our national security, which has become a focus of policy since the terrorist attacks on the World Trade Center in 2001. Recent advertisements in the press and TV by the Bush administration try to link use of marijuana with aiding terrorism.[23] In January 2002, the Office of National Drug Control Policy (ONDCP) unveiled its $10 million ad campaign that piggybacks the issue of drugs with the new focus on terrorism since the September 11 attacks.[24] The television commercials linking drug use to terrorist activity debuted during the 2002 Super Bowl. "It's despicable and dangerous," said Ethan Nadelmann, executive director of the Drug Policy Alliance. "When you start labeling tens of millions of Americans as accomplices to terrorists or de facto murderers, you are creating and stirring an atmosphere of intolerance and hate-mongering that ends up being destructive and dangerous to the broader society."[25] It isn't just policy advocates who are skeptical about this propaganda. According to one public-interest journal, "The Super Bowl ads received a resounding thumbs-down from political columnists, editorial writers, entertainers, and citizens across America."[26]

The advertisements have no basis in fact, and will backfire as the truth seeps out. Half of the marijuana used in the U.S. is produced domestically. Most domestic marijuana is probably used locally, within the state which it is grown. The rest is imported, mostly from Mexico and Canada. Neither of these countries is associated with terrorism. Thus trying to link marijuana use or sales with terrorism is a prevarication. In fact, a person is more likely to contribute to the finances of terrorists by buying a pair of sneakers made in Indonesia or gassing up with petrochemicals from Saudi Arabia, Kuwait, or Iraq. In fact, U.S. refiners purchase the majority of UN-authorized Iraqi oil imports.[27]

The ads are only a small part of the new "drugs-equal-terror" campaign. The spurious link between marijuana and terrorism is being used to increase the antidrug budget. Recently, DEA administrator Asa Hutchinson played up the drugs-terror connection in pushing a $1.7 billion budget request.[28] Using fear of terrorism to influence public opinion sets a dangerous precedent and creates polarization in society. Once opened, these wounds are slow to heal. The cynicism connected with this campaign is blatant. While the government is linking marijuana use to terrorism, its main antimarijuana campaign seems to be the arrest and prosecution of medical-marijuana patients and their providers. These actions directly contradict public sentiment. In a Zogby poll commissioned by the NORML in November 2001, 61 percent of respondents opposed the arrest and jailing of nonviolent marijuana smokers.[29]

8

Sociological Aspects

Americans ask, "What about our children?" but they forget that virtually any kid—in any city, town or suburb—who wants to try drugs can find them easily right now. And still others say, "What about the message it would send?" but forget that our current response—insane anti-drug efforts like "Just Say No" and "This Is Your Brain on Drugs," along with our incredibly cruel laws—send far worse messages: that kids are stupid, that drug users are less than human, and that people who do no harm to others deserve to lose their freedom.[1]

—Ethan Nadelmann and Jann Wenner

Marijuana use is a victimless action; there is no victim who wishes to report the crime to the police after the substance is used. To enforce the marijuana laws, the police have used such undercover methods as entrapment, informers, wiretaps, and surreptitious entry. This type of law enforcement creates tension and distrust in citizens who have to deal with the authorities, leading to alienation.[2] Now federal agencies are attacking medical users and suppliers who are "out," or more public.

A 1982 NAS study put its finger on the contempt that many young people have for the marijuana laws, noting that because they see "no rational basis for the legal distinction between alcohol and marijuana [they] may become cynical about America's political institutions and democratic processes."[3] Unfortunately, these laws breed not just cynicism but criminals. Most people, particularly juveniles who are arrested for marijuana, have no prior criminal record.[4] An arrest at this young age can indelibly alienate a person from law-enforcement authorities. In the case of the marijuana laws, the symbolic value of lawbreaking is further enhanced by the widespread belief that the state has overreacted to the marijuana "menace." The NAS study commented, "Young users, who are often otherwise law-abiding people, are subject to an arrest record, or even a prison term, with implications extending into many aspects of their lives."[5]

Since the enactment of a federal ban on scholarships and loans to marijuana offenders attending school, the reach of these laws has stretched considerably. The Bush administration has chosen to strictly enforce an amendment to the Higher Education Act, denying federal loan money to approximately 87,000 students, including 30,000 students in the 2002-2003 academic year.[6] These numbers have tripled since the 2000-2001 academic year.[7] In England, the Joseph Roundtree Foundation conducted an in-depth study that compared the attitudes of young drug users with nonusers regarding authority and law enforcement.[8] The study found that recreational drug users were only slightly less trusting of authority figures in general, with similar levels of trust for teachers, doctors, and parents as their nonusing counterparts. The biggest difference in opinion between the two groups was with respect to police and law enforcement. Recreational users had a significantly lower level of trust and respect for police and law enforcement specifically.[9]

"This disrespect has continued as the average age of marijuana users has risen," says John X., a marijuana user for twenty years. Neither consumers nor dealers—nor cultivators—feel that they are acting immorally or violating society's mores. Said one marijuana farmer, "I don't feel that I'm violating society's mores any more than a brewer of good beer or a wine maker. Laws that infringe on an American's right to life, liberty, and the pursuit of happiness deserve to be broken."[10]

In the 1980s, many police shared a similar view. "The people we are arresting for marijuana cultivation are not criminal types. People don't seem to take it too seriously," said Fresno Police Lieutenant Dailey in 1982.[11] Joe, a 71 year old marijuana dealer living in Mann County, California (who has never been arrested), said: "I don't feel any more criminal than those who were selling alcohol during Prohibition."[12] The police view has changed since they started profiting from the drug war. Now they take marijuana much more seriously and count on marijuana arrests to fill their extra-budgetary wish list.[13]

Users feel they are harassed because of lifestyle and recreational pursuits. Friends and relatives of arrestees also develop cynicism toward law enforcement because they view the marijuana laws as unjust and based on ignorance and misinformation.

Most politicians publicly revile drugs as being antithetical to so-called traditional American values. Marijuana users know that these statements are false and ignorant, particularly since so many politicians of both the left and right have had to admit to "youthful indiscretions." This causes a breach between users and the political establishment. If there were no laws prohibiting marijuana use, smokers and law-enforcement authorities would have no quarrel with each other. Instead, the laws have created a class of criminals.

Tim L., a graphic artist living in the San Francisco Bay Area, described the police-state mentality that these laws create in society. He recalled:

> I was vacationing in Venice, California. I was on the boardwalk by the beach and had just pulled a joint out of my jacket. I saw two bicyclists coming towards me, so I put the unlit joint back in my jacket. The cyclists were wearing shorts and only when they pulled out their badges did I realize they were police. They searched me illegally and found the joint and wrote me a citation. I said to them, "It's a good thing that you've cleared up all the rapes and murders in L.A. so that you have time to concentrate on important cases such as this." They mumbled that it was part of their job, somebody has to do it, and rode off. As they were leaving the scene, one of the cops said:
>
> "Why do you think they call it dope?" And I thought to myself, "Why do you think they call you pigs?"[14]

Some people who have tried marijuana are deterred from entering law enforcement because they do not wish to be called upon to enforce the marijuana laws. Some police departments have difficulty recruiting enough trainees because such a large proportion of potential candidates cannot comply with entry requirements about marijuana usage. Police enforcing these laws are often demoralized because their limited time and budget is used to enforce frivolous laws while serious crimes go unsolved. This mismanagement of resources has spurred the home secretary in England, David Blunkett, to reclassify cannabis, lowering the amount of police time spent on marijuana law enforcement.[15] Britain's cannabis policy is considered the most stringent in Europe; while this change in policy stops short of decriminalization, it is intended to more accurately match the amount of police time spent on marijuana with both the scientific evidence and public perception of its seriousness as a crime.[16]

Some police use marijuana themselves, opening the door to blackmail, payoffs, and bribery. Officers' attitudes toward the law and its enforcement are corrupted. As splashed across the headlines of city after city, police are not immune to the lure of quick profits while enforcing criminal penalties for victimless actions.

The harm that marijuana laws cause individuals is exacerbated by the damage the laws do to society. Thousands of marijuana-related arrests lead to long-term incarceration every year. Imprisonment leads to breakdown of families—and can spell psychological and economic disaster for loved ones. The marijuana laws ruin the lives of productive members of society.

Because so much emphasis has been placed on eradicating marijuana use, families often become polarized on the issue, creating an unhealthy home life. Pot smokers who used to hide their marijuana for fear their parents would turn them in now hide it from their children for the same reason, or because they might lose custody of their children if the children inadvertently mention the marijuana use to a legal authority or hostile parent or guardian. Children who grow up in such families usually know their parents are hiding something from them, thus creating major barriers to open communication within the family.

As long as marijuana remains contraband, there is no way for the government to regulate its sale. Under the current black market, it is actually easier for kids to buy pot than it is for them to get alcohol or tobacco, hardly a desirable outcome.

Parent groups regularly complain to authorities that marijuana is more available than alcohol to their junior high and high school children. The laws forbid store owners to sell alcohol or tobacco to minors, so teenagers need to use phony IDs or find an adult willing to buy liquor or cigarettes for them. However, marijuana may be only a phone call or bicycle ride away. Some youngsters grow secret marijuana gardens, while others burglarize growers' plots. Since marijuana is outside the regulatory system, parents have no legal recourse, unless they wish to start criminal proceedings against their children's suppliers (often their children's friends), which would cause great dissension within the family.

Marijuana is not the first popular recreational drug that the government has tried to prohibit. Alcohol prohibition brought with it a black market to supply the public's demands. As the government stepped up enforcement, stronger criminal gangs were needed to defy the laws. Some crime families functioning today started by distributing alcohol during Prohibition. When the ban ended, the criminal organizations diversified into other fields. By increasing law-enforcement efforts rather than introducing a civil regulatory system, the government is creating an environment conducive to the growth of criminal groups. The attempt at alcohol prohibition was a failure. It never succeeded in any of its goals. First, it failed to prevent distribution of alcohol. Second, because of the laws people's habits changed. Since beer, a mild intoxicant, was no longer available, people used whiskey, a much more concentrated intoxicant. From a harm-reduction viewpoint, this was a disaster. Beer was no longer available because it was much more profitable to sell whiskey.

Some of the most creative young entrepreneurs have entered the marijuana business because of its potential high profits. Running a successful operation requires management skills, innovation, initiative, financial continuity, and integrity. Their career choice is a loss for society because these bright people have dropped out of the mainstream economy.

The skewed lifestyles based on high-risk, high-profit enterprises exacerbate economic and social distortions in society. Most people who earn a living through marijuana are never apprehended. This leads to erosion of the work ethic and the feeling among those not in the business that crime is easy and that it does pay.

Society reacts to this by increasing the vigilance of enforcement and the penalties for offenders. The results are tragic, for these more stringent policies bring us closer to being a police state. Since such a large percentage of the population uses marijuana and there are no victims to file criminal complaints, entrapment and other covert actions are necessary to find the lawbreakers.

The government, which is intent on maintaining the marijuana laws and on increasing penalties, has polarized the scientific community in the process. On several occasions, North American governments have chosen to ignore unbiased, scientific, sociological, and health-related marijuana studies. The LaGuardia Report in 1943 found marijuana to be a benign substance; in 1972, the Shafer Commission called for decriminalization. The 1972 LeDain Report, a Canadian study of marijuana in society, also called for the legalization of cannabis. The 1982 NAS Study and the 1999 Institute of Medicine Report also called for changes in marijuana policy, but were ignored. Canada's Parliamentary Report, issued in 2002, recommended legalization. The Canadian government is seriously considering this report.[17] The members of these committees were able to study the issues without the pressures of constituencies. Apparently no North American head of state has had the inclination or courage to act upon the logical conclusions of these commissions. As we will see in chapter 9, European countries have been rapidly altering policy to a harm-reduction model more aligned with these findings.

Probably the most serious sociological problem that the marijuana laws create is the potential for discriminatory enforcement. Since so much of the population nationwide uses marijuana, it is impossible for police to enforce the law in all neighborhoods. Marijuana laws are often used to harass members of minority groups or those citizens with alternative lifestyles. This has been a common practice since the first marijuana laws were enacted in the United States. In 1982, Dr. Jerome Skolnik commented: "The marijuana laws have become an extension of police discretion—whether or not someone is a criminal is a matter of police discretion. They are looking for anything to catch bad people."[18] This policy has altered little since that time. While an estimated 20 percent of marijuana smokers in the U.S. are black or Hispanic,[19] almost 60 percent of marijuana offenders in federal prisons in 1997 were black or Hispanic.[20] State arrest and incarceration rates are similarly skewed.[21]

When the first modern antimarijuana laws were enacted in southern and southwestern states, the psychopharmocological nature of marijuana was of secondary importance to legislators. The laws were initiated because of fears about the people who used cannabis: young Mexican-American and black males. In 1931, the *New Orleans Medical and Surgical Journal,* in language characteristic of the era, wrote, "The debasing and baneful influence of hashish and opium is not restricted to individuals but has manifested itself in nations and races as well. The dominant race and most enlightened countries are alcoholic, whilst the races and nations addicted to hemp and opium, some of which once attained to heights of culture and civilization, have deteriorated both mentally and physically."[22]

In certain areas of the United States in the 1930s, the fear of marijuana and its users amounted to hysteria. "These areas mostly coincided with concentrations of Mexican immigrants who tended to use marijuana as a drug of entertainment or relaxation. . . . Legal and

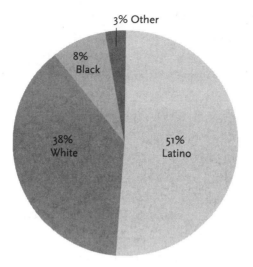

3% Other

8% Black

38% White

51% Latino

Who Are the Feds Incarcerating? Over half of federal marijuana prisoners are Latino. Given that Mexico is the largest single importer of marijuana to the U.S., that number may not be entirely surprising. Still, federal emphasis on the Mexican border probably leads to a disproportionate arrest rate of Latinos.

Source: U.S. Dept. Of Justice, Bureau of Justice Statistics, *Federal Drug Offenders, 1999 with Trends 1984-1999* (NCJ 187285, Aug. 2001) p.11 Table 8.

medical officers in New Orleans began studies on the evil, and within a few years published articles claiming that many of the region's crimes could be traced to marijuana . . . for they believed it to be a sexual stimulant, which removed civilized inhibitions."[23]

In 1935, the *New York Times* asserted:

Marijuana, perhaps now the most insidious of our narcotics, is a direct by-product of unrestricted Mexican immigration. Easily grown, it has been asserted that it has recently been planted between rows in a California penitentiary garden. Mexican peddlers have been caught distributing marijuana cigarettes to schoolchildren. Bills for our quota against Mexico have been blocked mysteriously in every Congress since the 1924 Quota Act. Our nation has more than enough laborers.[24]

Through the early 1960s, using marijuana was regarded as a near-subversive act, a ploy of the communist conspiracy to destroy the country. According to the 1982 NAS study:

> It was not until the 1960s that most Americans became aware of marijuana. The political and cultural protests of that period focused public attention on young people, their lifestyles, and their use of drugs, including marijuana. . . . For the first time marijuana use was not restricted to minority groups and fringe elements of society: many of the new users were native-born middle-class white college students. Without doubt, the political and cultural context in which marijuana emerged as an issue of national concern has strongly influenced the subsequent policy debate about its use.[25]

Now, in order to prevent the marijuana laws from imploding, the criminal system is targeting patients and their suppliers. It is shoring up the weakest front of the marijuana laws.

DARE to Think for Yourself

In 2000, the Drug Abuse Resistance Education (DARE) program taught its curriculum to 25 million children in the U.S. and 8 million children in other countries.[26] Local governments, states, and the federal government spent about $750 million on DARE in 1994.[27] Police officers attempt to teach kids the "Three R's": Recognize, Resist, and

Report. They are encouraged by DARE officers to turn in friends and family because "they are sick and need help."[28] DARE programs don't mention that the "help" will be in the form of prison sentences for their parents, foster homes for the kids, and asset forfeiture for the family.

All of the major research on the effectiveness of DARE shows that it has no impact on the rate of drug use by children.[29] In 1999, the University of Kentucky conducted a follow-up study on the DARE program. Researchers found that graduates of DARE are as likely to use drugs in high school as those who have not gone through the program.[30] A similar study conducted in England followed about 1,000 students who had been in either a standard drug education curriculum or the DARE program. It evaluated the effect of the curriculum at sixth grade, and then again at age twenty. In 1999, the study reported that the two groups displayed no significant differences in actual drug usage, attititudes toward drugs, or self-esteem issues.[31] In an article on their study in *Consulting and Clinical Psychology,* the researchers stated that "in no case did the DARE group have a more successful outcome than the comparison group."[32]

In "A Different Look at DARE," the researchers point out that "despite its huge popularity, and hundreds of millions in tax revenue and private contributions, no evidence exists that DARE keeps kids off drugs.[33] It concludes that, "Two federal agencies that evaluate drug education programs do not recommend DARE. DARE is known to be a failure based on at least half a dozen independent peer reviewed studies."[34]

Social Consequences of Marijuana Prohibition

The potential harm from marijuana is outweighed by the documented damage that the marijuana laws cause society. Millions of arrests, hundreds of thousands of people incarcerated each year, thousands of lives ruined—an alienated, polarized society and hypocrisy that extends from the cop on the beat to the highest levels of government. In the end, society has nothing positive to show for its efforts.

The war on pot has been a disaster for our society. Consider the price society is paying:

- Children turning in their parents
- Parents turning in their kids
- Friends turning in their friends
- Families ripped apart
- Billions of dollars wasted each year to enforce marijuana laws
- Six million people a year under court supervision[35]
- Property valued at more than $1 billion seized each year
- Millions of seriously ill patients denied safe, inexpensive relief
- Farmers denied a chance to join the growing worldwide hemp industry
- The humiliation and loss of privacy inherent in widespread drug testing

For what is society paying? To stop people from using a natural herb? Marijuana is cheaper and more plentiful than ever. Nearly everyone knows the government is lying about pot. Even the DEA's own judge agrees that it is wrong to keep marijuana from sick people.[36] Yet the government remains frozen on the issue of marijuana, perpetuating the same lies in a feeble effort to cover up the lies of the past.

It is time for change. If society wants to have some control over marijuana, then it must be legalized and placed within a civil regulatory format.

**Partial List of Contributors to "Partnership
for a Drug Free America" by Amount of Contribution***

Chairman's Circle ($50,000 and over)

Bristol-Myers Squibb Foundation

Eastman Kodak Company

Johnson & Johnson

Metropolitan Life Foundation

The Procter & Gamble Fund

Gold Medallion ($25,000 to $49,999)

Bayer Corporation

The Coca-Cola Company

Consumer Healthcare Products Association

The GE Fund

General Motors Foundation

GlaxoSmithKline

H. J. Heinz Company Foundation

Kimberly-Clark Foundation Inc.

Major League Baseball

McNeil Consumer & Specialty Pharmaceuticals

Merrill Lynch & Company Foundation, Inc.

Novartis Consumer Health, Inc.

Perrigo Company

Pfizer Foundation, Inc.

Pharmacia Corporation

Schering-Plough Corporation

Wyeth

* Taken verbatim from the Partnership for a Drug Free America website's Corporate Sponsor list, www.drugfreeamerica.org.

Silver Medallion ($15,000 to $24,999)
Bechtel Foundation
DaimlerChrysler Corporation Fund
ExxonMobil Foundation
PACCAR Foundation
The UPS Foundation
The Xerox Foundation

9

Why Marijuana Isn't Legal

We have spent the last few chapters discussing the marijuana laws' costs to society. These laws are so expensive to maintain and deleterious to society that it is irrational for the U.S. to keep them. Yet the laws have withstood efforts to eliminate them for more than thirty years. In fact, in many states and at the federal level, the penalties have increased during this time. Why is this issue disrespected so by politicians and the rest of government? Who is standing in the way of marijuana law reform, and why are they doing it?

When the first Marijuana Tax Act was enacted in 1937, several lobbying groups pushed for its passage. The pharmaceutical companies were interested in seeing it made illegal so they could sell more of their new drugs to treat many of the same medical conditions for which marijuana was efficacious. Alcohol prohibition had just ended and the industry was flexing its muscles. If marijuana remained legal, many people would never drink but would use marijuana instead.

The police had a profound interest in marijuana. On a federal level, all the prohibition cops were about to be laid off since alcohol was no longer illegal. They would either find other police work or join the

Depression bread line. In the U.S.'s South and Southwest, police viewed marijuana as the "Devil's Weed." Mexican-Americans and blacks, as well as entertainers and other undesirables, used it. Making the herb illegal would make it easy to harass them.

The growth of the marijuana law penalties and of the substance's popularity has made it even more important to the law-enforcement community. In 2000, about 734,500 people were arrested for marijuana offenses[1] out of an estimated total of 14 million arrests that year.[2] Five percent of the criminal justice system's resources were used to persecute marijuana users. When I say the criminal justice system, I am describing the broad industry. It includes the police, state's attorneys, judges and other court personnel, jailers ("call us corrections officers"), probation and parole departments, drug-rehabilitation clinics, and all the other redundant personnel who exploit both the victims of the drug war and the taxpayers.

There are over 2 million people in prison or jail today.[3] About 4 percent of the people incarcerated were convicted of marijuana possession or sales.[4] Cannabis-law offenders make up a greater proportion of prisoners because of the harsh drug laws. So the 5 percent figure is accurate for arrests, but is a very conservative figure regarding the number of people who are in custody for violating marijuana laws. For instance, as we mentioned in chapter 2, 20 percent of federal prisoners are imprisoned for marijuana violations.[5] Collectively, marijuana prisoners populate a small city and need the basic services that any community requires.

Even more frightening for our society, the police and prison industries have sunk deep tentacles throughout the civilian economy. Private prisons will always clamor for more inmates. If filling the prisons requires harsher laws to ensnare more citizens, so be it. The companies will lobby for their enactment after propagandizing citizens into hysteria regarding crime. Manufacturers also have a stake in the issue. More police equipment, including vehicles, weapons, and protective gear, will be needed. More prisoners translates into more prisons. Building them has been a growth industry since the Reagan administration.[6]

Vendors, who supply food, clothing, and other provisions to prisons, also have an interest in a rising prison population. So do companies that exploit prison labor. Marijuana laws bring better-quality prisoners to the government-run housing complexes. Higher-quality prisoners make better employees for the compulsory/slave labor market, no matter the consequences to individuals or society.

In 1937, when marijuana was criminalized, there were estimated to be about 50,000 marijuana users in the U.S. Now there are at least 27 million.[7] That's a 50,000 percent increase in 65 years. The War Against Marijuana is one of the greatest policy failures in U.S. history. However, it has been a tremendous success for the marijuana-prohibition industry. As the number of marijuana users has increased, a greater proportion of the police budget is allocated to its suppression. Rather than cutting the same pie into different-sized slices, the system is allocated more funding, a bigger pie to divide.

Marijuana is an excellent foil in an eradication campaign. No matter how harsh the penalties and how much money is thrown at the effort, the war against marijuana cannot succeed. People like to change their consciousness and will take great risks to do it. Therefore, the amount of money that can be used to fight the marijuana war is limited only by the criminal system's ability to persuade, cajole, or threaten the budgetary bodies.

Analyzing the Figures

In 2000, 647,000, or 88 percent, of the 735,000 people arrested for marijuana were busted for simple possession. Only 88,000 were arrested for dealing, and most of these busts were for small retail amounts.[8] These figures show how ineffective the government's efforts against traffickers have become. It isn't in the system's interest to stop the trade, just to poach victims from it.

The justice system of the fifty states and the federal government, including the cops, courts, prisons and after-court systems such as probation, parole, and drug rehabilitation, costs taxpayers a total of about $160 billion each year.[9]

If marijuana were legal or civilly regulated, there would be 5 percent fewer cops, cop cars, criminal court cases, and prisoners. The change in policy would result in a direct saving of $16 billion a year. It is for this very reason that there is opposition to civil regulation by special-interest groups. These groups look upon the savings to the government and the taxpayers as job loss and loss of profits, in much the same way the cigarette industry looks at regulations concerning cigarette use.

The DEA, FBI, and other antidrug federal agencies and their state counterparts will be the hardest hit when marijuana prohibition ends. Marijuana accounts for 46 percent of all drug arrests.[10]

Once marijuana is placed on a civil regulatory system, most employees of these agencies will become redundant. In 2002, the DEA employed about 9,400 people.[11] Almost every law-enforcement unit, every local police department, and every district attorney's office devotes manpower to enforce marijuana laws. These people would be redundant. Most "drug rehabilitation" clinics, whose marijuana clients are referred by the courts, would close. Judges, prison guards, and all the corporations providing services or buying prison labor would be affected.

The Proof of Proposition 36, the Substance Abuse and Crime · Prevention Act

In 2000, voters in California approved an initiative allowing people who are arrested for simple possession of drugs to go through a rehabilitation program rather than through the court process that would result in prison.[12] Since the program was initiated, most agree it has been very successful. It results in less recidivism and is considerably cheaper than imprisonment. Who were the main opponents of the initiative on the ballot arguments sent out by the state? The self-interested parties: judges, prison guards, and police.[13] It was a bread-and-butter issue to them. Since its enactment, Prop. 36 has become a model for other states. It strives to lower the rate of drug use without jailing people. Initial reports on its enactment have been positive.[14]

State Analysis: The Major Provisions of Proposition 36[15]

- **Changes sentencing laws,** effective July 1, 2001, to require offenders convicted of "nonviolent drug possession," as defined, to be sentenced to probation and drug treatment instead of prison, jail, or probation without treatment. Excludes some offenders, including those who refuse treatment and those found by courts to be "unamenable" to treatment.

- **Changes parole violation laws,** effective July 1, 2001, to require that parole violators who commit nonviolent drug possession offenses or who violate drug-related conditions of parole complete drug treatment in the community, rather than being returned to state prison.
- Requires that eligible offenders receive up to **one year of drug treatment** in the community and up to six months of additional follow-up care.
- Establishes certain **sanctions for offenders** found unamenable for treatment or who violate the conditions of probation or parole. Permits courts (for probationers) and Board of Prison Terms (for parole violators) to require **offenders to participate in training, counseling, literacy, or community service.**
- Requires that treatment programs be **licensed or certified** by the state Department of Alcohol and Drug Programs (DADP). Requires **offenders to pay** for their treatment, if they are reasonably able to do so.
- **Appropriates state funds for distribution to counties** to operate drug-treatment programs and provide related services.
- Requires DADP to **study the effectiveness** of the measure and to **audit county expenditures.**

In the official election guide, the argument opposing the proposition was written by Stephen V. Manley, president of the California Association of Drug Court Professionals. The ballot argument opposing Prop. 36 was signed by John T. Schwarzlose, president of the Betty Ford Center; Alan M. Crogan, president of the Chief Probation

Officers of California; and Thomas J. Orloff, president of the California District Attorneys Association.[16]

Notice that all of these people and the organizations they represent have a self-interest in the continuation of the marijuana laws. Their arguments turned out to be unfounded and wrong. It must be embarrassing for the experts to have their theories tested and revealed as false. It bares their arguments as job-preserving but detrimental to society.

Law-enforcement personnel are motivated to keep marijuana illegal for two other reasons. The first is that employees of the criminal justice system want to retain the right to persecute marijuana users. They resent any other approach to the issue. Some of these people are addicted to the adrenaline of the cops-and-robbers formula. They may also like the sense of authority and power. Sadistic attitudes of messing with peoples' lives may also come into play.

The second reason is a self-righteous attitude, often based on myths or bias. Some law-enforcement personnel choose to remain ignorant rather than educate themselves about the issue. They disapprove of the lifestyles of marijuana users who represent society's liberal mores, and feel distinct from mainstream culture. Rather, they see themselves as guards herding it, the front line protecting it from anarchy. They think this gives them the right to dictate society's policies. Drug Czar Walters is an extreme example. In the face of solid medical evidence of the efficacy of marijuana, some of it based on research by agencies he works with, he denies any medical uses.[17]

Marijuana users transcend ethnic and economic boundaries and cannot be stereotyped in the same way as other drug users. Police perceive that many marijuana users are smarter than other types of criminals, and resent marijuana users' attitude that smoking marijuana does not make them criminals. Cocaine, methamphetamine, and opiate users are often dysfunctional people who sit lower in the hierarchy than non-users. However, this isn't necessarily so with cannabis. The cannabis smoker may be successful and happy. In the puritanical mind of the marijuana-law enforcer, these people don't deserve to be happy and should be punished for their use.

Alcohol and Pharmaceutical Interests

Today the criminal system is the greatest supporter of prohibition. However, it is not the only industry with a self-interest in preserving marijuana prohibition. The alcohol industry has been a consistent supporter of "drug abuse" groups.

When marijuana is legalized and more people have a choice of intoxicants, it is probable that many people who have abstained from cannabis and used alcohol as a substitute will change their habits. This will be a big blow to brewers and distillers. Brewers and distillers have an interest in protecting their monopoly in the marketplace. Corporations with interests in the industry were early contributors to quasi-independent organizations such as Partnership for a Drug Free America. Alcohol companies have turned their attention to the local level as well. Their sponsorship of DARE programs and other local antidrug crusades is an important part of the fear campaign about marijuana and youth.

In 1937, when marijuana was criminalized, the pharmaceutical industry viewed cannabis as a threat to the sales of their analgesics and medicines. Most of the large pharmaceutical companies made preparations of "Indian Hemp," extracts of marijuana varieties with a high THC content.[18] Marijuana had been available in over-the-counter medicines since the last quarter of the nineteenth century.[19] However, pharmaceutical chemists had not discovered the molecule and thus were unable to synthesize it.[20] Bayer had already synthesized salicylic acid and created aspirin.[21] Starting with the natural analgesic made from the bark of the weeping willow plant, scientists made a standard synthetic preparation, which was much more profitable to produce and market. It provided the consumer with a consistent standardized dose of the drug.

Over the years, marijuana's threat to the pharmaceutical industry shrank as new and better synthetics appeared on the market. The memory of marijuana as a medicine and analgesic faded from the public mind. The only evidence that remained current in the 1960s seemed to be peoples' anecdotal experiences.[22] For instance, in the late 1960s I had a friend who used it for menstrual cramps. In 1978, Robert Randall pioneered the federal government's "Compassionate Use Program."[23] At one time, the program served twenty patients.[24] Only seven remain alive. The HIV-AIDS epidemic removed the lid of secrecy regarding marijuana. The program was flooded with applications from HIV patients, since marijuana was anecdotally known as an anti-emetic. Rather than admitting more patients, the first Bush administration opted to close the program to new applicants in 1992. The program has not admitted new patients since then.[25] Almost all research into marijuana remains funded by U.S. government agencies. Their grant process favors research that focuses on forensic or harmful aspects of marijuana use.

The International Cannabinoid Research Society (ICRS) is a membership society of researchers.[26] Most of its members are grant holders who are funded by government agencies, such as the DEA and NIMH. At the 1999 ICRS symposium, Dr. Jeffrey Guy of the British company GW Pharmaceuticals announced research into medical applications of cannabis for multiple sclerosis.[27] In 2000, GW Pharmaceuticals floated its initial public offering (IPO) of stock. Since then, major pharmaceutical research companies have taken the therapeutic aspects of cannabis more seriously. At the 2002 convention, more papers dealt with medical and analgesic aspects of cannabinoids than in any previous year.[28]

Some companies are studying twisted cannabinoid molecules to deal with specific acute conditions. However, natural marijuana varieties contain useful combinations of cannabinoids for many analgesic and medical problems. These medicines could be grown at home or on farms.

Pharmaceutical companies view natural marijuana as competition for their patented, proprietary medicines. The pharmaceutical companies have a renewed self-interest in keeping marijuana illegal so that people will purchase patented medicines instead of the natural herbs.

California's Proposition 215:
Medical Use of Marijuana Initiative Statute

In 1996, the voters of California passed a law through the initiative process to regulate medical marijuana within the state. The law is commonly called Prop. 215, named for its number on the ballot.

In summary, the law provides for the following:

- Patients and defined caregivers who possess or cultivate marijuana for medical treatment recommended by a physician are exempt from criminal laws which otherwise prohibit possession or cultivation of marijuana.
- Physicians who recommend use of marijuana for medical treatment shall not be punished or denied any right or privilege.

- The measure is not to be construed in order to supersede prohibitions of conduct endangering others or to condone diversion of marijuana for nonmedical purposes.[29]

It seems simple enough—physicians who recommend marijuana, medical-marijuana users, and their providers are not to be harassed by the law. Almost everyone in the state understood what the law meant. The only exceptions were in the criminal system. The unions and professional organizations representing criminal system personnel had been opposed to passage of the initiative. In the state voters pamphlet, James P. Fox, president of the California District Attorneys Association, wrote the official opposition, which said:

READ PROPOSITION 215 CAREFULLY IT IS A CRUEL HOAX

The proponents of this deceptive and poorly written initiative want to exploit public compassion for the sick in order to legalize and legitimatize the widespread use of marijuana in California.

Proposition 215 DOES NOT restrict the use of marijuana to AIDS, cancer, glaucoma and other serious illnesses.

READ THE FINE PRINT Proposition 215 legalizes marijuana use for "any other illness for which marijuana provides relief." This could include stress, headaches, upset stomach, insomnia, a stiff neck . . . or just about anything.

NO WRITTEN PRESCRIPTION REQUIRED

EVEN CHILDREN COULD SMOKE POT LEGALLY!

Proposition 215 does not require a written prescription. Anyone with the "oral recommendation or approval by a physician" can grow, possess or smoke marijuana. No medical examination is required.

THERE IS NO AGE RESTRICTION. Even children can be legally permitted to grow, possess and use marijuana . . . without parental consent.

NO FDA APPROVAL NO CONSUMER PROTECTION

Consumers are protected from unsafe and impure drugs by the Food and Drug Administration (FDA). This initiative makes marijuana available to the public without FDA approval or regulation. Quality, purity and strength of the drug would be unregulated. There are no rules restricting the amount a person can smoke or how often they can smoke it.

THC, the active ingredient in marijuana, is already available by prescription as the FDA approved drug Marinol.

Responsible medical doctors wishing to treat AIDS patients, cancer patients and other sick people can prescribe Marinol right now. They don't need this initiative. [30]

Associations that signed the ballot opposition to Prop. 215 included the California State Sheriffs, the California Police Chiefs, the California Narcotic Officers, and the California Peace Officers. In addition, Attorney General Dan Lundgren, Californians for Drug-Free Youth, the California DARE Officers Association, and Drug Watch International officially opposed Prop. 215.

Mr. Fox closed his arguments with the statement, "this initiative allows unlimited quantities of marijuana to be grown anywhere . . . in backyards or near schoolyards without any regulation or restrictions. This is not responsible medicine. It is marijuana legalization."[31] Apparently, Mr. Fox has changed his opinion about how liberal Prop. 215 really is. Immediately after the proposition passed, the District Attorneys Association attempted to limit the quantity of medicine patients could legally possess.

Notice that all the people who opposed medical marijuana on the ballot are drug warriors whose income is dependent on the continuation of the war on marijuana users. None were concerned that they were opposing distribution of medicine to patients. Their only real interest was the jobs issue. All of them were unconcerned about prohibition's cost to society and using their positions of authority only in their self-interest.

Once the law was passed, state Attorney General Dan Lundgren, later defeated as a gubernatorial candidate and since faded into oblivion, promulgated a state policy of restrictive interpretation of the law: in other words, a policy of harassment.[32] Since 1996, thousands of medicinal users have had to face court because of mean-spirited criminal policies. For the most part, juries and appellate courts have upheld the rights of patients rather than recognize the uncivil arguments of the prosecuting attorneys. Still, many patients plead out because they had neither the energy nor the finances to wage a legal battle to protect their rights.

Each year since Prop. 215 was enacted, uncompassionate district attorneys have indicted medical-marijuana patients. Did District Attorney McGregor W. Scott of Shasta County really think that he was protecting society when he prosecuted medical patient Rick Levin and his wife, Kim, for possession and cultivation?[33] District Attorney Ambrust was proud to prosecute Marvin Chavez, a caregiver for thirty patients in Orange County.[34] These prosecutors claimed that the law was vague and wanted the courts to interpret it.

The police and district attorneys' opposition to medical marijuana stems from typical hard feelings of people who fear losing work and authority. They try to assert their importance and feel aggrieved at their demotion. They lash out at victims. In these cases, it has been the poor and sick. Certainly the government's actions were not

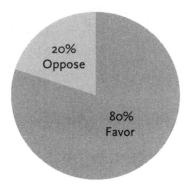

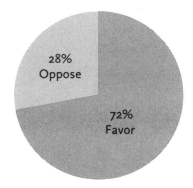

Medical Marijuana: More Popular Than Any Politician. Eighty percent say medical marijuana should be legal.

Over 70% Think Recreational Users Should Get Fines, Not Jail. By an overwhelming majority, Americans agree with changing the law from jail time to a fine, which is essentially decriminalization. A number of states currently have decriminalization laws in effect, but federal policy favors harsh penalties.

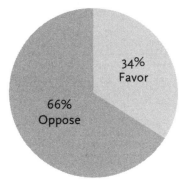

Complete Legalization Favored by One-Third. Legalization, or civil regulation, is a complete reversal of America's policies. The number of people in support of completely legalizing marijuana has doubled since 1986.

Source: Time/CNN Poll in Time vol.160, no. 19 (Nov. 4, 2002)

serving society. Instead these officials were harassing citizens and wasting taxpayers' money. These officials put their own self-interest before serving the public. District attorneys who persecute medical-marijuana users should be driven from office by the voters for incompetence and squandering public funds.

Finally, in July 2002, in the *CA v. Mower* case, the California Supreme Court found that patients using marijuana had rights equal to those using other prescription drugs:

> As we shall explain, we conclude that the Court of Appeal was correct in concluding that section 11362.5(d) does not confer the "complete" immunity from prosecution claimed by defendant. But we also conclude that, in light of its language and purpose, section 11362.5(d) reasonably must be interpreted to grant a defendant a limited immunity from prosecution, which not only allows a defendant to raise his or her status as a qualified patient or primary caregiver as a defense at trial, but also permits a defendant to raise such status by moving to set aside an indictment or information prior to trial on the ground of the absence of reasonable or probable cause to believe that he or she is guilty.[35]

Six years after the enactment of the statute, the court agreed with Pebble Trippet's reasoning in her amicus brief.[36] After the court rendered its decision, she wrote,

> According to a unanimous Supreme Court focusing on patients' rights, medical marijuana users with a doctor's recommendation are "no more criminal" than prescription drug users. A physician's marijuana recommendation for a medical purpose is

the equivalent of and should be treated the same as for any other prescription drug, in order to apply equal protection under the law (Health & Safety Code 11362.5). *CA v. Mower* changes everything. Marijuana is medicine. The Supreme Court has restored medical freedom and first class citizenship (the equivalent of prescription access) to cannabis patients, who are by law to be protected, instead of prosecuted and punished as criminals. This is a principled equal rights ruling, based on the purpose as stated in the language of the law ("To ensure that patients and their primary caregivers who obtain and use marijuana for medical purposes upon the recommendation of a physician are not subject to criminal prosecution or sanction"). [37]

As a result of this court decision, medical-marijuana users are presumed to be innocent, just like any other prescription drug user. It will be the state's burden to prove that there was any other purpose for the possession or cultivation of marijuana.

Success at the local level and success in both trial court and in appeals has changed the environment for medical-marijuana users. Before this decision, the courts and the voters had enlarged the rights of medical-marijuana patients. Juries were reluctant to convict medical-marijuana users, and many cases were dropped because the prosecution realized it could not get a conviction. Still, prosecutors wasted time and resources pursuing the cases. This boondoggle is over.[38]

Meanwhile, marijuana was wending its way through the political process. Some of the local elections proved that marijuana could be a potent issue. In San Francisco, there was a runoff election for district attorney in 2000. Terence Hallinan was the candidate preferred by the marijuana dispensaries. They enrolled about 6,000 new voters during the registration period. The new voters turned to Hallinan in overwhelming proportions. He won the election by fewer than 2,000 votes out of 200,000 cast.[39] Marijuana users turned the tide and elected the new DA.

In Mendocino County, California, in 2000, the district attorney initiated a case against medical provider Ken Hayes, who was accused of growing about 900 plants to help provide for some of the 1,200 patients registered at his dispensary.[40] The district attorney, Mike Mullens, not only lost the case, but in the next election, held in 2002, he was ousted by an electorate tired of his policies, which squandered money on marijuana while showing little initiative in serious crimes such as domestic violence and even murder.[41] In California's March 2002 primary elections, in the heart of the "Emerald Triangle," both the Humboldt County sheriff and the district attorney lost their posts because of their intolerant attitude toward marijuana.[42]

Recent polls indicate that the public is tired of the war on marijuana users and ready to cast ballots based on this issue.[43] The success of the medical-marijuana initiatives in nine states as well as local government approval of medical-marijuana facilities proves the point.[44]

The Harm-Reduction Paradigm: The European Example

In 1976, the Dutch government opted out of the prevailing worldwide drug policy of eradication, punishment, and rehabilitation.[45] In its place, the Netherlands substituted the nascent policy of "harm reduction."[46]

An alcoholic who substitutes beer for hard liquor could be considered in the first step of a harm-reduction paradigm. That person is substituting a less potent and thus less dangerous drug for a more potent one.

In the same way, the Dutch government separated drugs into two categories: "soft" and "hard." Marijuana and hashish were placed in the soft drug category. Virtually all other drugs were considered hard drugs. Since that time, the government has tolerated "coffeeshops," in which small quantities of marijuana can be purchased for on-site or off-site consumption.[47]

Rather than jailing addicts, the government offers them treatment on demand. Mobile methadone clinics offer the desperate addict a "fix" of methadone. The reasoning is that it is one day off of heroin. The mobile units offer clean needles as well as treatment on demand. The government figures that being addicted is no reason to contract AIDS. After all, for most people addiction is a transient condition; infection is terminal.

Goals of Harm Reduction

Since the Dutch introduced the idea, the logic of the policy, as well as its effectiveness in dealing with drug problems, has spread to the rest of Europe. The policy of the European Union is changing from crime and punishment to harm reduction.[48] Canada has also adopted this policy and is legalizing marijuana as this book is being written.[49]

Abstinence has proven to be impossible to achieve and the attempt to enforce it is more harmful to society than the controlled substances themselves. The goal of harm reduction is to guide people away from the most harmful substances, to ones that offer the least harm to the individual and society. Under this policy, addiction and harm are differentiated.

The most widely used addictive substance is generally available to the public, is not very harmful, and is not regulated at all. Most adults enjoy its use while it helps them with their productivity. Caffeine is rarely abused by children, has no black market or violence associated with its use, and is advertised freely.[50]

Alcohol, which has a moderate degree of addictiveness, is a dangerous drug that society regulates with a close eye because of the harm associated with it. It is a great mental debilitator, and is associated with heart, kidney, and liver disease. Its use is associated with death from accidents as well as homicides. The total number of alcohol-related deaths is recorded at more than 100,000 annually.[51] However, the total is probably much higher. With inconsistent civil regulation and spotty education, abuse of alcohol is still a major problem in this country.[52]

Tobacco is moderately addictive. It was first identified as a dangerous substance of abuse in 1604 in King James's "Counterblaste to Tobacco."[53] It is now the cause of more than 400,000 deaths in the U.S. annually, as well as a major cause of other health problems.[54]

Marijuana is slightly addictive. Under the paradigm of harm to society and to the individual, marijuana fits just behind caffeine in its safety. There are no deaths reported from its use.[55]

The danger of overtoking or eating one brownie too much is a feeling of tiredness resulting in a healthy nap. Aside from hysteria on the part of prohibitionists, there are virtually no mental conditions associated with its use.

From a harm-reduction paradigm, people who substitute marijuana for alcohol have a dramatic reduction of harm. Epidemiological reports show that marijuana use is not associated with a higher morbidity rate.[56] Unlike alcohol addiction, most users use only occasionally, and when most heavy users decide to quit or reduce use, they are usually able to change their use pattern without professional help.

The Advantages of the Harm-Reduction Paradigm

The United States has some of the harshest antidrug laws in the world. Fifteen percent of the arrests in the U.S. are for drugs.[57] As the number of people arrested each year grows, drug use fluctuates a bit, with a general upward trend.[58]

The drug laws are the result of racism, fear of "bohemians" and special interests. They are not the result of a reasoned, thought-through strategy with the goal of benefiting society. It requires a realistic assessment of the situation and the impact of regulations on it to create a well-designed program that will reduce harm. The criminal system has not and cannot meet those goals. It has been tried for more than seventy years and has been a total failure in meeting society's aims.[59]

The U.S. has already had success with the harm-reduction strategy. Tobacco reduction has been such a success in this country that countries all over the world have emulated it. Since the mid-1990s, European countries have carried harm-reduction policies even further by eliminating advertising for tobacco products. With the success of tobacco harm reduction in their countries, the Europeans see civil regulation of marijuana and harm-reduction policies, rather than criminal statutes, as the way to deal with substance abuse.

Implicitly, we all accept the statement, "If there's a profit in it, somebody will be willing to supply it, even at great risk." Unless there is a major change in human nature, this will be true for the foreseeable future. This is the reason that the War on Drugs can't work by limiting supply as long as demand remains unquenched. However, a drop in demand creates an incentive to stop production because of falling prices and less profitability.

The European nations and Canada are accepting the harm-reduction model for several reasons. The first is that the model they had tried, criminalization, doesn't work. On the other hand, harm reduction is cost-effective, especially in terms of long-term social policy. It is also more effective in containing the problem and not exacerbating secondary effects of substance use, such as unsafe streets and long-term health effects, including hepatitis and AIDS.

Today, the primary intoxicant in the U.S. is alcohol. Both federal and state governments apply vice taxes on it, and their budgets figure those taxes in. However, it is associated with many deaths each year, either from diseases associated with it or from accidents and homicides. Its relationship to additional health risks, violent behavior, and crime is well established.

Marijuana is not associated with a higher morbidity rate or with violence. In fact, the only violence associated with most illegal substances is the result of prohibition. The violence is not about the substance, it's about the combination of money and illegal activities.

10

How to Legalize Marijuana

This book has described the harm that the laws do to individuals and society, and the motives behind them. If this book has helped you determine that marijuana should not be illegal, then it has met its first goal. Understanding the situation is the beginning of a process that will lead to change.

The next step is to act upon your beliefs. Just knowing about the injustice and harm created by marijuana prohibition does not bring us closer to a system of civil regulation. Every progressive change in the marijuana laws was the result of the active effort of diverse groups of people putting in a range of efforts. I have tried to get others involved. It has been a bittersweet experience. For years I despaired at the lack of political responsibility of many marijuana smokers who don't vote or make any contribution to changing the law. Because of political apathy, marijuana wasn't even on the political radar.

However, my mood has changed to inspiration as I see the thousands of people all over California pressing the medical-marijuana issue and Prop. 215. Even with the threat of enforcement of federal marijuana laws, brave people continue to provide medicine to their friends and neighbors who are in need. You can't get more active than that. Being around this political movement is an uplifting experience.

Not everyone can make the sort of commitment and risk that providers must take. However, no matter where you live or what you do for a living, you can help change the marijuana laws. Whatever level of commitment you want to make, whether or not you want to come out, you can help change the marijuana laws.

Many people don't have the time in their schedules, or are not comfortable performing volunteer work. Perhaps you are concerned about being recognized or you are in a delicate situation. There are still several valuable services you can perform. The first is to make a financial contribution to the cause. Sometimes I daydream that the 20 million regular users each decided to give $10 to a marijuana-law-reform organization—$200 million—or 2 million people contributed $100, the price of a quarter-ounce of high-quality weed. Marijuana would be legal in about a week, 100,000 marijuana prisoners would be freed from jails and prisons, 6 million people would lose their criminal histories regarding the substance, and users would no longer be relegated to the status of outlaws.

I was shocked to learn that only 2 to 3 percent of Americans contribute to political campaigns.[1] Some people make no contributions to any charity. I hope that you, the reader, feel differently about your responsibility to society.

I have a relative who keeps up on the news, rants and raves about the social situation at family gatherings, but contributes no money or time to change the situation. He apparently thinks his main patriotic duty is to vote. That's not enough to change policy. Voting is just the beginning. If he doesn't have the time or inclination to lend his talents to change the situation, he can write a check to help others work in his interest.

We know that not every marijuana user has the intelligence and foresight that you do. You know how important it is to support organizations fighting for your rights. You may think your contribution won't make much of a difference to a large organization, but to win, this must be a collective effort. Even if your contribution is small, it becomes a formidable war chest when added to other contributions. Local organizations have much smaller budgets than national ones. Your contribution will have greater significance to a local organization that is working the home turf.

Your choice of which organization to support is not as important as actually making the contribution. It is also important that you give generously. Remember—you're not doing organizations a favor by contributing funds; they are helping you by fighting for your rights. The least you can do is contribute.

Most of the people directly affected by the marijuana laws aren't going to give $10. And it is also unlikely that 2 million people will each contribute $100. It is really up to you, a small group of socially conscious people, to create change.

Think of this: if you buy an ounce every month and spend $300 on it, your medicine or your pleasure is costing you a little less than $75 a week. If you send just one check a year for $75, less than 2 percent of your yearly marijuana bill, you will take a tremendous step toward changing the legal environment. Still, $75 is not a lot when you consider the stakes. Could you do it four times a year? Contributing money takes the least effort.

Here are some other things you can do to change the laws:

- Write letters to newspapers regarding specific articles, op-eds, and editorials. Praise them when you agree and damn them when you disagree. Give a reasoned argument for your opinion. Don't attack the writer.

- Write, e-mail, or fax newspaper reporters when you have an opinion about their articles. Offer to provide them with accurate information. Provide them with Internet sources for information. Offer to act as a second opinion for quotes to balance police and government statements.

- Write your local, state, or national legislators. You may actually sway local legislators with meaningful dialogue. Sometimes you can meet them for a face-to-face and develop a working relationship.

- Talk with your friends and relatives about the issue. See if they are willing to help legalize. How about a letter-writing party, and a check to the marijuana organization of your choice? People can write letters to the usual gang of suspects, the media, whether TV, radio, or print, as well as local, state, and national politicians. The media uses and respects well-composed letters from the Internet and by e-mail. However, politicians and officials respect snail mail more than e-mails. Faxes are effective, too.

- Join a marijuana-law-reform organization. Participate in their actions and events. Be part of a group taking action in one way or another to change the marijuana laws.

- Volunteer to work a table for a marijuana organization at an event.

- Graphics, writing, public relations, telephone work, banner making, lobbying—virtually any skill you have can be used in an organization. If you don't think you have any skills but would like to learn some, volunteer as an intern. At first you will be doing necessary go-for work, but you will be given more responsibility as your skills improve.

· Start a local chapter. Nothing going on where you live? Open a chapter of one of the national organizations in your community. You will be surprised by how much support you will get if you work well with people.

· Support organizations that are trying to change the laws by buying their products at events and markets. Don't need another marijuana lei? Just make a contribution.

Annotated List of Marijuana Organizations

Here is a list of organizations that are fighting to change the marijuana laws. Some of them post volunteer opportunities or actions that can be taken. Several offer newsletters and all have informative websites. These groups focus on different aspects, from legislative and policy reform and legal support to grassroots action and offering direct support to medical-marijuana patients or current marijuana prisoners. Donations to many of these organizations are tax deductible.

Adopt A Green Prisoner Project (ADOPT)
Will Foster
P.O. Box 12063
Oakland, CA 94604
willfoster@AdoptAGreenPrisoner.org
www.adoptagreenprisoner.org

American Alliance for Medical Cannabis (AAMC)

JCavana857@aol.com

www.letfreedomgrow.com

Americans for Safe Access (ASA)

A campaign of the Cannabis Action Network

1678 Shattuck Ave., #317

Berkeley, CA 94709

510-486-8083 phone

510-486-8090 fax

info@safeaccessnow.org

www.safeaccessnow.org

Cannabis Action Network (CAN)

1678 Shattuck Ave., #317

Berkeley, CA 94709

510-486-8083 phone

510-486-8090 fax

cannabisaction@cannabisaction.net

www.cannabisaction.net

Cannabis College

O.Z. Achterburgwal 124

P.O. Box 10952

1001 EZ Amsterdam Netherlands

sponsors@cannabiscollege.com

www.cannabiscollege.com

Cannabis MD and Lifevine Foundation

Located in Washington state

www.cannabismd.com

Drug Policy Alliance
www.drugpolicy.org
Select the contact information
for the location nearest you:

New York
70 W. 36th St.
16th Floor
New York, NY 10018
212-613-8020 phone
212-613-8021 fax
nyc@drugpolicy.org

New Jersey
119 S. Warren St.
1st Floor
Trenton, NJ 08608
609-396-8613 phone
609-396-9478 fax

Washington, D.C.
925 15th St., N.W.
2nd Floor
Washington, D.C. 20005
202-216-0035 phone
202-216-0803 fax
dc@drugpolicy.org

New Mexico
1227 Paseo de Peralta
Santa Fe, NM 87501

505-983-3277 phone
505-983-3278 fax
nm@drugpolicy.org

San Francisco
2233 Lombard St.
San Francisco, CA 94123
415-921-4987 phone
415-921-1912 fax
sf@drugpolicy.org

Sacramento
1225 8th St., Suite 570
Sacramento, CA 95814
916-444-3751 phone
916-444-3802 fax
sacto@drugpolicy.org

Legal Affairs
717 Washington St.
Oakland, CA 94607
510-208-7711 phone
510-208-7722 fax
legalaffairs@drugpolicy.org

Drug Reform Coordination Network (DRCNet)
2000 P St., N.W., #210
Washington, D.C. 20036
202-293-8340 phone

202-293-8344 fax
drcnet@drcnet.org
www.drcnet.org

Drug Sense
P. O. Box 651
Porterville, CA 93258
800-266-5759
greer@drugsense.org
www.drugsense.org

Families Against Mandatory Minimums (FAMM)
1612 K St., N.W., Suite 700
Washington, D.C. 20006
202-822-6700 phone
202-822-6704 fax
famm@famm.org
www.famm.org

Forfeiture Endangers American Rights (FEAR)
265 Miller Ave.
Mill Valley, CA 94941
415-389-8551 phone
888-FEAR-001 toll-free
www.fear.org

Green Aid
PMB #172
484 Lake Park Ave.

Oakland, CA 94610

888-271-7674

www.green-aid.com

International Association for Cannabis as Medicine (IACM)

Arnimstrasse 1A

50825 Cologne

Germany

+49-221-9543 9229 phone

+49-221-1300591 fax

info@cannabis-med.org

www.cannabis-med.org

Marijuana Policy Project (MPP)

MPP Foundation

P.O. Box 77492

Capitol Hill

Washington, D.C. 20013

202-462-5747 phone

202-232-0442 fax

info@mpp.org

www.mpp.org

Media Awareness Project (MAP Inc.)

A Drug Sense project

P.O. Box 651

Porterville, CA 93258

800-266-5759

mgreer@mapinc.org

www.mapinc.org

Medical Marijuana Patients Union (MMPU)
P.O. Box 2059
Fort Bragg, CA 95437
activism@mmpu.org
www.mmpu.org

Multidisciplinary Association for Psychedelic Studies (MAPS)
2105 Robinson Ave.
Sarasota, FL 34232
941-924-6277 phone
888-868-6277 toll-free
info@maps.org
www.maps.org

National Organization for the Reformation of Marijuana Laws (NORML)
(chapters in various states with individual websites)
1600 K St., N.W.
Suite 501
Washington, D.C. 20006-2832
202-483-5500 phone
202-483-0057 fax
norml@norml.org
www.norml.org

November Coalition
795 S. Cedar
Colville, WA 99114
509-684-1550 phone

moreinfo@november.org

http://november.org

Oakland Cannabis Buyers Cooperative (OCBC)

P.O. Box 70401

Oakland, CA 94612-0401

510-832-5346 phone

510-986-0534 fax

ocbc@rxcbc.org

www.rxcbc.org

Sonoma Alliance for Medical Marijuana (SAMM)

P.O. Box 216

Sebastopol, CA 95473

707-522-0292 voice mail

docknapp@sonic.net

www.samm.net

Students for Sensible Drug Policy (SSDP)

1623 Connecticut Ave., N.W.

3rd Floor

Washington, D.C. 20009

202-293-4414 phone

202-293-8344 fax

ssdp@ssdp.org

www.ssdp.org

Voter Power

333 S.W. Park Ave.

Portland, OR 97205
503-224-3051 phone
503-224-3065 fax
john@voterpower.org
www.voterpower.org

Wo/Men's Alliance for Medical Marijuana (WAMM)

309 Cedar St., #39
Santa Cruz, CA 95060
info@wamm.org
www.wamm.org

11

Ed Rosenthal on His Arrest

The day that I was arrested, February 12, 2002, I entered a new phase of activism. I do not look upon my indictment as one for criminal activity. I was seized because the U.S. government is committed to senseless wars. Sometimes the U.S. is at war with foreign countries, sometimes with its own citizens. I am one of the more than 730,000 people arrested for marijuana in 2002. So in that respect, I don't take it personally.

However, in spite of the fact that I am just another body to count in the statistics of the War On Marijuana Users, more specifically, medical-marijuana users, I have to take it personally because of the threat of extended jail time. No one likes looking at the future and seeing a path that leads directly to jail. Just as in Monopoly®, you don't get to pass "GO."

I realize that the two paragraphs above may seem to be totally contradictory. They are the two edge points that go through my mind every day. What I am certain of is that serving the medical-marijuana patients was a blessing for me. I know that a system that punishes people who serve the sick is evil. I know that I helped to extend the lives of people and helped others to live more pleasant lives. I find it ironic that the individuals in charge of the federal government think that medical-marijuana caregivers and their patients are the most threatening drug users on the horizon. I wonder, do they live in the same world we do? Don't they and their loved ones get sick? Are they immune from pain and suffering?

How many times have you heard, "Thank God you have your health." For the most part, we take our health for granted. However, all of us have been struck with the flu or another temporarily debilitating condition. Then we realize how difficult it can be to sit up, cross the room, or wend our way to the toilet. Imagine being a person living with those handicaps into the foreseeable future.

In the San Francisco Bay Area, where I live, AIDS has been a scourge. Until the protease inhibitors were invented, testing positive for HIV placed you on the short path to Terminal Station. Then a life-saving cocktail of drugs was discovered. The only problem is that to take them you need anti-emetics. Marijuana is the best one. However, it is widely illegal, so you must grow your own, or you may be able to go to an alternative health center that provides it if you live in a state with a medical-marijuana initiative. This is the reality for thousands of Californians and other Americans. These peoples' lives hang in the balance of the medical-marijuana laws.

There were twelve people living in four houses on my street when I moved in. Four of them died from AIDS within ten years. Had Skip, the last to die, lived just a year longer, protease inhibitors would have snatched him from death to a near-normal life. All of these people used marijuana to ease their pains and stop the nausea they frequently experienced.

My friend and noted author, Tom Flowers, died from complications from arthritis. Until the day he died he used cannabis as medicine both internally, swallowing "mari-pill"—capsules filled with trim and olive oil—and also using a vaporizer. Externally, he used marijuana salves. They always provided relief.

My mother died from a wasting disease just a few years before Tom. She was all skin and bones when she died, weighing less than seventy pounds. Although she knew I used it, she never dared to try a piece of a cookie, Marinol (the synthetic THC), or any other cannabis preparation. She was too scared by the propaganda to use the one medicine that could have made her feel better and encouraged her appetite.

Since Skip died, I have met many people who lived to receive the newer cocktails and are still around and kicking. Although Congress has decreed that marijuana has no medical value, these patients know better. They consider marijuana a part of their medicinal regimen, along with the protease inhibitors. Any law that prevents such people from getting medicine is immoral and a crime against humanity. These laws may be enforceable, but they lack the authority of legislation. They are themselves criminal, in the same way that slavery and segregation were.

I had the good fortune to attend a speech given by Tony Serra, the courageous attorney, a number of years ago. His talk was about the psyche of a criminal defense attorney. He compared a good attorney to a Viking warrior living in Valhalla. In the afterlife, brave warriors are in combat all day. During the evening their wounds heal and they are able to fight again the next day. Valhalla represented not only victory, but the ability to struggle, to be hurt, and to recover from wounds and struggle once again. Victory and peace were short-lived and very recreational, because the call to battle would soon interrupt them, and when it came, it drew all.

This speech connected the dots for me. I had never understood how a warrior could be a spiritual person, practicing a form of meditation. This seemed to be a contradiction to me. How could a person naturally take the stance of the warrior and still be a spiritual person? Serra's speech helped me make my decision to be an expert witness, to do hand-to-hand combat with the DEA and other prosecutors for peoples' lives.

I felt comfortable in that position for more than ten years. I was able to do good, was stimulated intellectually, and got to hang out with some very interesting and some very smart people. I was working in court without a law degree. The courtroom is the epitome of warriors doing battle. And like the warriors in Valhalla, I walked away even if the prosecutor's victim didn't. I don't like losing, so it was a good thing that I worked with talented lawyers and was able to help people during some of the darkest hours of the drug war. It was a quite satisfying feeling.

Proposition 215 opened up new opportunities for me to serve. My first efforts were to help get the proposition on the ballot. There are quite a few people who can say, "If I didn't do this . . . the prop wouldn't have happened or wouldn't have won." I am one of them. In addition to helping with strategic work, I was appointed chairperson of the Alameda County 215 Committee. We gathered the second-highest number of signatures in California. In addition, we were the only county committee able to raise most of our own funds without support from the central organization.

After the proposition passed and the dispensaries were set up, Oakland city officials asked me to assist the patients and the medical community. It was sort of like deciding to do expert testimony. I decided to step in the water after the sincerest of people bid me to come in. After being a warrior, kindness and love seemed like a good karmic balance. I could use the expertise I had gained in the service of the sick and dying. In return I would be able to work with some truly compassionate people.

I believe my work with the medical dispensaries helped people plagued by the most heartbreaking illnesses. When I visited the dispensaries I always left with blessings from patients that surrounded me in a bubble of love. It wasn't uncommon for a person to credit me for his or her very life.

The people of the San Francisco Bay Area have a very enlightened attitude toward both medical and recreational use of marijuana. This is the area where Prop. 215 originated and one of the first areas in the country where marijuana voter blocs have tipped local political races. Our local governments, both in San Francisco and Oakland, continue to encourage dispensaries to serve patients.

The court first considered my case in January 2003. My pre-trial motions, which were based on faults in the search warrant and constitutional issues, were denied. Then, at the trial, the judge refused to let me present my theory of the case—that I was doing nothing illegal since I was carrying out Oakland, California's medical marijuana policy as an officer of the city. Even if the city's interpretation of the policy was incorrect, I should have been protected under an estoppel defense: I had been misled by authorities. I was not allowed to present this evidence to the jury, or put most of my witnesses on the stand. The judge also usurped my attorney's direct examination of one of the two witnesses I was permitted. I was found guilty on all charges.

The post-trial reaction by the jury was unprecedented. Nearly half of the jurors publicly denounced the justice of their own verdict and called for a new trial. The attention that the case has received by the national and international media is encouraging; it shows that the contradictions within the marijuana laws are a topic of true concern to the American public, and it has helped to mobilize a new national conversation on the issue. It has also solidified the support of the vast majority of the people for medical marijuana.

Meanwhile, the legal work regarding my case continues. The lawyers are filing motions, complaints and appeals. Investigations are continuing and the case is inching forward. To fight this case I have again taken the stance of the warrior. Nobody knows what will happen at the end of this lawsuit. I have already learned quite a bit. First of all, and perhaps most importantly, I learned how much I am loved and how the whole community has come to medical marijuana defendants with an outpouring of concern and support. This is extremely important. Second, I have learned that the stance of the warrior and the caregiver are often the same. I hope I meet your expectations.

For more information about Ed Rosenthal's arrest and subsequent trial, check the websites of activist organizations Green Aid (www.green-aid.com) and Americans for Safe Access (www.safeaccessnow.org).

Appendix 1

Proposition 215: California Medical Use of Marijuana Initiative Statute

The law reads:

SECTION 1. Section 11362.5 is added to the Health and Safety Code, to read:

11362.5. (a) This section shall be known and may be cited as the Compassionate Use Act of 1996

(b)(1) The people of the State of California hereby find and declare that the purposes of the Compassionate Use Act of 1996 are as follows:

(A) To ensure that seriously ill Californians have the right to obtain and use marijuana for medical purposes where that medical use is deemed appropriate and has been recommended by a physician who has determined that the person's health would benefit from the use of marijuana in the treatment of cancer, anorexia, AIDS, chronic pain, spasticity, glaucoma, arthritis, migraine, or any other illness for which marijuana provides relief.

(B) To ensure that patients and their primary caregivers who obtain and use marijuana for medical purposes upon the recommendation of a physician are not subject to criminal prosecution or sanction.

(C) To encourage the federal and state governments to implement a plan to provide for the safe and affordable distribution of marijuana to all patients in medical need of marijuana.

(2) Nothing in this section shall be construed to supersede legislation prohibiting persons from engaging in conduct that endangers others, nor to condone the diversion of marijuana for nonmedical purposes.

(c) Notwithstanding any other provision of law, no physician in this state shall be punished, or denied any right or privilege, for having recommended marijuana to a patient for medical purposes.

(d) Section 11357, relating to the possession of marijuana, and Section 11358, relating to the cultivation of marijuana, shall not apply to a patient, or to a patient's primary caregiver, who possesses or cultivates marijuana for the personal medical purposes of the patient upon the written or oral recommendation or approval of a physician.

(e) For the purposes of this section, "primary caregiver" means the individual designated by the person exempted under this section who has consistently assumed responsibility for the housing, health, or safety of that person.

SECTION 2. If any provision of this measure or the application thereof to any person or circumstance is held invalid, that invalidity shall not affect other provisions or applications of the measure that can be given effect without the invalid provision or application, and to this end the provisions of this measure are severable.

Appendix 2

Acronyms and Abbreviations

Governmental Organizations, Offices, or Studies

BJS	Bureau of Justice Statistics (a division of the U.S. DOJ)
CIA	Central Intelligence Agency
DADP	Department of Alcohol and Drug Programs
DASIS	Drug and Alcohol Services Information System
DAWN	Drug Abuse Warning Network (a division of SAMHSA)
DEA	Drug Enforcement Administration
FBI	Federal Bureau of Investigation
FDA	Federal Drug Administration
IACOP	International Association of Chiefs of Police
IMF	International Monetary Fund
IRS	Internal Revenue Service
LeDain Report	1972 Canadian marijuana study
NAFTA	North American Free Trade Agreement
NAS	National Academy of Sciences
NCHS	National Center for Health Statistics
NHSDA	National Household Survey on Drug Abuse
NHTSA	National Highway Traffic Safety Administration

NIAAA	National Institute on Alcohol Abuse and Alcoholism
NIDA	National Institute on Drug Abuse
NIMH	National Institute of Mental Health
NRC	National Research Council
OAS	Office of Applied Studies (a division of SAMHSA)
ODCCP	Office for Drug Control and Crime Prevention
ONDCP	Office of National Drug Control Policy
SAMHSA	Substance Abuse and Mental Health Services Administration
Shafer Commission	National Commission on Marijuana and Drug Abuse, 1972
TEDS	Treatment Episode Data Sets
UN	United Nations
U.S. DOJ	U.S. Department of Justice
U.S. GPO	U.S. Government Printing Office
USDA	United States Department of Agriculture
WHO	World Health Organization

Private or Nonprofit Organizations

AAMC	American Alliance for Medical Cannabis
ADOPT	Adopt A Green Prisoner
ASA	Americans for Safe Access
CAN	Cannabis Action Network
DARE	Drug Abuse Resistance Education
DRCNet	Drug Reform Coordination Network
FAMM	Families Against Mandatory Minimums
FEAR	Forfeiture Endangers American Rights
HIA	The Hemp Industries Association

IACM	International Association for Cannabis as Medicine
ICRS	International Cannabinoid Research Society
MAP Inc.	Media Awareness Project
MAPS	Multidisciplinary Association for Psychedelic Studies
MMPU	Medical Marijuana Patients Union
MPP	Marijuana Policy Project
NORML	National Organization for the Reform of Marijuana Laws
OCBC	Oakland Cannabis Buyers Cooperative
SAMM	Sonoma Alliance for Medical Marijuana
SSDP	Students for Sensible Drug Policy
WAMM	Wo/Men's Alliance for Medical Marijuana

Notes

Introduction

1. California NORML, "Marijuana Violations for Year 2000 Hit All Time High, FBI Report Reveals," California NORML News Release (Oct. 22, 2001).
   http://www.canorml.org/news/calmj2000 arrests.html [Nov. 2002].

2. NORML Foundation, "NORML Report on Sixty Years of Marijuana Prohibition in the U.S.," (1997), Part II.
   http://www.norml.org/index.cfm?Group_ID=4428 [Oct. 2002].

3. For an interesting commentary on changes of consciousness, refer to Aldous Huxley, *Doors of Perception* (New York: Harper & Row, 1970).

1 Preserving Our Constitutional Rights

1. Excellent books discussing religion and marijuana are Ernest Abel, *Marijuana: The First 12,000 Years* (New York: McGraw Hill, 1980); and Chris Beneath, Lynn Osburn, and Judy Osburn, *Green Gold: The Tree of Life* (California: Access Unlimited, 1995).

2. The U.S. Court of Appeals for the Ninth Circuit ruled on February 2 that under the Religious Freedom Restoration Act of 1993, Rastafarian defendants should be allowed to show that they use marijuana for bona fide religious reasons in their defense against charges of possession of marijuana. Source: *U.S. v. Bauer,* No. 94-30073, 96 C.D.O.S. 756, 1996 WL42240 (9th Cir. 1996).

3. For example, DEA agents raided Steve McWilliams, co-director of Shelter from the Storm, on September 22, 2002. The first raid of its kind in San Diego, it came after McWilliams received a handwritten letter warning him to destroy his small personal-use medical garden or face federal charges. Local officials had approved McWilliams's garden. It contained 28 plants, and served a few severely ill medical-marijuana

patients. The raid followed McWilliams's involvement in a public protest. McWilliams was subsequently arrested on federal charges in October, and now faces a possible 5-year mandatory minimum sentence. Source: NORML Foundation, "Feds' Prosecution of Outspoken California Medi-Pot Patient for 20 Plants Raises Free Speech Questions NORML Head Charges" (Oct. 17, 2002).
http://www.norml.org/index.cfm?Group_ID=5437 [Dec. 2002].

4. Richard Glen Boire, *Marijuana Law* (Berkeley, CA: Ronin Publishing, 1992), p. 30.

5. Many law-enforcement agencies rely on forfeitures for a major part of their funding. Between 1985 and 1991, the Justice Department collected more than $1.5 billion in illegal assets; in the next five years, the Justice Department almost doubled this intake, depositing $2.7 billion in its Asset Forfeiture Fund. In 1999, more than $600 million was deposited in the Justice Department's Asset Forfeiture Fund alone. The department has regularly exhorted its attorneys to make "every effort" to increase "forfeiture production" to avoid budget shortfalls. Multijurisdictional drug task forces "expect to have to rely increasingly on asset forfeitures for future resources." After Utah voters closed the forfeiture spigot in 2000, many drug units there expected downsizing or termination to follow. Source: Eric D. Blumenson and Eva Nilsen, "The Next Stage of Forfeiture Reform," *Federal Sentencing Reporter* 14(2) (Sept./Oct. 2001), p. 76; http://www.fear.org/menuidx2.html [Oct. 2002].

6. NORML Foundation, "Sixty Years of Marijuana Prohibition," 1997, Part III.

7. A five-year review on multijurisdictional drug control task forces showed an 89 percent increase in asset seizures by task forces between 1988 and 1992, noting that such seizures "provide resources to task forces that have experienced decreased funding." (Source: Justice Research and Statistics Association, *Multijurisdictional Drug Control Task Forces: A Five Year Review 1988–1992*, 23 (Oct .1993).) "Drug cops may be reined in: Congress is likely to make it harder for the government to take money, homes, cars and other items in drug cases" (Source: William E. Gibson and Lisa J.

Huriash, *Orlando Sentinel* (Apr. 11, 2000) at A-1 citing the Senate Judiciary Committee.)

8. U.S. Dept. of Justice, Bureau of Justice Statistics (U.S. DOJ, BJS), *Sourcebook of Criminal Justice Statistics 2000,* Table 5.33, citing annual reports from the Administrative Office of the U.S. Courts.

9. On May 14, 2001, the Supreme Court voted unanimously against the use of a medical-necessity defense in marijuana cases. This ruling disallows the mention of medical circumstances in federal marijuana trials, inhibiting the full presentation of evidence.

10. Dale Gieringer, "Jury Convicts Keith Alden in First Federal Medical MJ Trial in S.F.," California NORML News Release (Feb. 11, 2002). http://www.canorml.org/news/aldenconvicted.html [Nov. 2002].

11. Ibid.

12. Americans for Safe Access (ASA), "Keith Alden Faces 20-year Mandatory Minimum," ASA Press Release (Nov. 14, 2002). http://www.safeaccessnow.org/article.php?id=227 [Nov. 2002].

13. Bruce Mirken, "Using Student Loans to Fight Drugs Is Counterproductive," *Charleston (WV) Daily Mail* (Jan. 1, 2002). http://www.mapinc.org/drugnews/403/n005/a07.html [Oct. 2002].

2 Criminal Innocents

1. California NORML News Release, "Marijuana Violations Hit All-Time High"; FBI Office of Uniform Crime Reports, "Crime in the United States—1995."

2. These are conservative figures. They don't include court costs and other government expenses. Source: *National Drug Control Strategy: FY Budget Summary for FY's 2001, 2002,* The White House.

3. Ibid.

4. FBI Office of Uniform Crime Reports, "Crime in the United States—1995," Section IV, pp. 207-8, Tables 4.1 and 29.

5. FBI Uniform Crime Reports, "Crime in the United States—2000," Section IV, p. 216, Tables 4.1 and 29; California NORML News Release, "Marijuana Violations Hit All-Time High."

6. Marijuana consumption, according to federal statisticians, averaged 811 metric tons the first half and 932 metric tons the second half of the 1990s, and was estimated to be 1,047 metric tons for 2000. Source: Office of National Drug Control Policy (ONDCP), *What American Users Spend on Illegal Drugs, 1998–2000.* For more information on marijuana consumption estimates, see Chapter 3, pp. 29-32.

7. The federal government has not reported on the age of marijuana arrestees for many years, but many states report about half such arrests are persons under 21 years of age. In California in 2001, 31 percent of 12,000 marijuana felony arrests and 47 percent of marijuana misdemeanor arrests were of persons under 20 years old. Source: California Department of Justice, *Crime and Delinquency in California 2001.*

8. The Shafer Commission's purpose was to investigate the increasing use of marijuana and make recommendations for governmental action. It was named for Raymond Shafer, former governor of Pennsylvania, who headed the commission. In March 1972, the commission issued its report, entitled *Marijuana. A Signal of Misunderstanding, the Technical Papers of the First Report of the National Commission on Marijuana and Drug Abuse,* government stock #5266-0002. The *Shafer Report* was a massive effort: 1,252 pages published in two volumes. It was widely hailed by human-rights activists, lawyers, and members of the medical community for its fair and logical conclusions and suggestions. President Nixon said that he tossed the report in a wastebasket without reading it. In an interview with on January 20, 1983, Governor Shafer said, "I am proud of that report. I stand by it, and I am satisfied that it helped to initiate change in the laws." Probably as a direct result of the recommendations of the report, thirteen states with 50 percent of the nation's population decriminalized marijuana to varying extents.

9. *The Shafer Report,* p. 693.

10. Edward Brecher, *Licit & Illicit Drugs: The Consumers Union Report on Narcotics, Stimulants, Depressants, Inhalants, Hallucinogens, and Marijuana* (New York: Little, Brown & Co., July 1974), p. 471.

11. At Donnie's sentencing, U.S. District Court Judge Elizabeth Kovachevich stated, "These guidelines are harsh, but harsher ones are coming. Soon someone is going to seek the death penalty for what you've done. This country is perhaps going overboard out of frustration with this drug problem." Source: Families Against Mandatory Minimums (FAMM). http://www.famm.org.

12. "Don Clark," *St. Petersburg Times* (Jan. 24, 2001) as cited by The November Coalition. http://www.november.org/thewall/cases/clark-d/clark-d.html [Oct. 2002].

13. Will Foster and Kimberly Sherrill, "Jacob Sink and Roy Sharpnack: A Story of Injustice," for Adopt A Green Prisoner Project website. http://www.adoptagreenprisoner.org/JSandRSinjustice.htm [Nov.2002].

14. Oakland Cannabis Buyers Cooperative website. http://www.rxcbc.org/ pactive.html [Nov. 2002].

15. In 2001, a total of 627,132 offense arrests were reported in the Uniform Crime Reporting Program's Crime Index for violent crimes. There were 723,627 arrests for marijuana in 2001. Eighty-eight percent of these arrests were for simple possession, not sale or manufacture. Source: FBI Uniform Crime Reports, "Crime in the United States —2001," Section IV, pp. 232-33. http://www.fbi.gov/ucr/cius_01/01crime4.pdf [Nov. 2002].

16. *The Shafer Report,* p. 816 (footnote 5).

17. International Centre for Prison Studies, "World Prison Brief: Highest

Prison Population Rates" (July 1, 2002).
http://www.kcl.ac.uk/depsta/rel/icps/worldbrief/highest_prison_
population_rates.html [Oct. 2002].

18. U.S. DOJ, BJS, *Prisoners in 1994* (NCJ 151654) and *Correctional Popula-tions in the United States* (NCJ 146413).

19. U.S. DOJ, BJS, *Prisoners in 2001* (NCJ 195189)
http://www.ojp.usdoj.gov/bjs/abstract/p01.htm [Oct. 2002].

20. U.S. DOJ, BJS, "Jail Statistics."
http://www.ojp.usdoj.gov/bjs/jails.htm [Oct. 2002].

21. U.S. DOJ, BJS, *Sourcebook of Criminal Justice Statistics 2000,* Table
6.50, adapted from tables provided by the Federal Bureau of Prisons.

22. U.S. DOJ, BJS, *Drugs and Jail Inmates,* 1989 (NCJ-130836).

23. U.S. DOJ, BJS, *Prisoners in 2001.*

24. U.S. DOJ, BJS, *Profile of Jail Inmates, 1996,* (NCJ 164620).
http://www.ojp.usdoj.gov/bjs/abstract/pji96.htm [Oct. 2002].

25. The Witherspoon Society, "Washington Office reports on rising prison
populations even as crime rates fall" (Oct. 2002).
http://www.witherspoonsociety.org/criminal_justice.htm [Dec. 2002].

26. U.S. DOJ, BJS, *Prisoners in 2000* (NCJ 188207).
http://www.ojp.usdoj.gov/bjs/abstract/p00.htm [Oct. 2002].

27 NORML estimates that the total number of marijuana arrests since 1965
passed the 10 million mark on July 20, 1995.

28. California NORML News Release, "Marijuana Violations Hit All-
Time High."

29. "Marijuana Arrests Near All-Time High in 2001," Marijuana Policy

Project (MPP) News Release (Oct. 28, 2002).
http://www.mpp.org/releases/nr102802.html [Nov. 2002].

30. "Special Release: Marijuana Arrests For Year 2001 Second Highest Ever Despite Feds' War On Terror, FBI Report Reveals," NORML News Release (Oct. 28, 2002).
http://www.norml.org/index.cfm?Group_ID=5444 [Nov. 2002].

31. "Marijuana Arrests Near All-Time High in 2001," MPP News Release.

32 In 1999, "[a]lmost one-third of defendants convicted of a drug offense in Federal courts were involved with marijuana," the largest percentage for any drug. Drug offenders have made up approximately 60 percent of federal prisoners between 1998 and 2001. Therefore, marijuana offenders make up 20 percent of the total federal prison population. Sources: U.S. DOJ, BJS, *Federal Drug Offenders 1999, with Trends 1984–99* (NCJ 187285).
http://www.ojp.usdoj.gov/bjs/pub/pdf/fdo99.pdf [Nov. 2002], p. 9; U.S. DOJ BJS, *Prisoners in 1999; Prisoners in 2000; Prisoners in 2001.*

33. U.S. DOJ, BJS, *Prisoners in 2001,* p. 14.

34. Chuck Thomas, "Marijuana Arrests and Incarceration in the United States," *FAS Drug Policy Analysis Bulletin,* issue 7 (June 1999).
http://www.mpp.org/arrests/fas61699.html [Nov. 2002].

3 Economic Costs

1. The marijuana industry is one of the only truly competitive industries in the United States. The price of the substance is determined solely by supply and demand. There is easy entrance and exit from the market; that is, anyone can become a dealer or quit dealing. There are no cartels or interests that control a significant percentage of market share (at least domestically); there are no monopolies or oligarchies as are found in most industries in the United States. Part of the price that consumers pay is a "premium" for the risk factor associated with pursuing an illegal enterprise. To make it worth the risk, there must be a higher profit potential

than in legal businesses or there would be no incentive to enter the market. The sellers are compensated directly by the government, since dealers pay virtually no taxes on their profits. In higher tax brackets, that alone could be significant. If the risk were eliminated through regulation, part of the premium now paid to dealers would be paid to the government as excise tax. Noneconomic factors associated with illegal enterprises would be eliminated, allowing for a significant drop in price.

2. "It has been observed that marijuana is one of the largest tax-exempt industries in the country today and regulation would end that exemption," *Report of the Task Force on Cannabis Regulation to the Center for the Study of Drug Policy–Regulation and Taxation of Cannabis Commerce* (Washington, D.C.: Dec. 12, 1981).

3. The federal tax on cigarettes is 11 percent of the retail price. State taxes are approximately the same amount at 10 percent. We presume that marijuana would be taxed at a higher percentage: double the rate for cigarettes. Sources: Campaign for Tobacco-Free Kids, "Federal Cigarette Tax Lower than Historical Levels," http://tobaccofreekids.org/research/factsheets/pdf/0092.pdf [Nov. 2002]; National Center for Chronic Disease Prevention and Health Promotion, "Trends in State and Federal Cigarette Tax and Retail Price, 1955–1995," http://www.cdc.gov/tobacco/research_data/economics/cigtax.htm [Nov. 2002].

4. Federal alcohol and tobacco taxes raised over $13 billion in fiscal year 1999, including about $7.7 billion from taxes on distilled spirits, beer, and wine and about $5.4 billion from taxes on tobacco. Source: Congressional Budget Office, "Index Tobacco and Alcohol Rates for Inflation." (Feb. 2001). http://www.cbo.gov/bo2001/bo2001_showhit1.cfm?index=REV 49 [Nov. 2002].

5. State sales taxes range between 4 and 8 percent. Source: The Sales Tax Clearinghouse. http://thestc.com/STrates.stm [Nov. 2002].

6. Possible new cannabis-related industries might include seed and nursery stock, specialized-growers supplies, cultural events, video and movie documentaries, nightclubs, and food-related products.

7. One can easily imagine that government agents might seek to entrap or frame an individual who has property or valuables desired by the government. Given the prosecution's leeway regarding entrapment, the government would be able to successfully pick on virtually any property holder in the United States.

8. In a huge proportion of marijuana cases, the defendants do not fight the charges in court. For instance, in 2000, 94 percent of persons facing federal charges chose not to contest the case, pleading guilty or no contest. Source: U.S. DOJ, BJS, *Sourcebook of Criminal Justice Statistics 2000*, Table 5.33.

9. Attorney Norman Kent said that in south Florida, "[f]elonies for simple possession start at $5,000 and felonies for growing start at $15,000." Source: Interview, July 8, 1996. Mr. Kent is a graduate of the Hofstra School of Law, a former law professor at Florida Atlantic University, and is currently in private practice in Ft. Lauderdale.

10. Personal communication from attorney. In 1981, this attorney quoted legal costs starting at $2,000. In the past two decades, the minimum cost for representation in wholesale distribution or conspiracy cases has increased to more than twelve times its 1981 rate.

11. Two billion dollars per year in legal billings for marijuana cases may be a conservative estimate for the start of the 21st century. In 2000, according to the FBI's annual Uniform Crime Reports, there were 735,000 marijuana arrests—88,450 for sale/manufacture, and 646,050 for possession. If half of those arrested for sale/manufacture hired private attorneys and paid an average of $15,000, and if only 10 percent of those arrested for possession hired private attorneys and paid an average of $7,500, the total billings for private attorneys defending marijuana cases would be just over $1 billion ($665 million to defend sale/manufacturing arrestees; $485 million to defend the marijuana

possession cases). The few cases that are appealed, with the intent of challenging the drug laws and their consequent enforcement practices on basic legal principles, can easily cost the defendant, and those who contribute to the defense fund, hundreds of thousands of dollars.

12 National Narcotics Intelligence Consumers Committee, "The Supply of Illicit Drugs to the United States" (Aug. 1995). In terms of dollar value, the domestic crop, which retails for 5 to 10 times the price of Mexican marijuana, far exceeds all imports. According to experts at *High Times,* probably 50 percent of the marijuana consumed in this country is domestic. Probably 10 million marijuana smokers regularly enjoy marijuana that they, their family, or their friends have grown.

13. U.S. Department of Agriculture (USDA), "Agricultural Statistics 2002," (Washington, D.C.: U.S. Government Printing Office [GPO]) p. ix-1, table 9.1.
http://www.usda.gov [Nov. 2002].

14. Ibid.

15. A single 1,000-watt lamp garden can produce an average of 6 pounds of pot per year, which is worth a gross of $12,000–$16,000.

16. Personal communication, April 8, 1996.

17. The 1961 United Nations Single Convention on Narcotic Drugs expressly recognized the distinction between marijuana and industrial hemp. This allows other member countries of the United Nations, such as Canada, Germany, and England, to grow hemp without breaking any international drug agreements. The U.S. imports hemp from these countries, but the 1970 Comprehensive Drug Abuse Prevention and Control Act effectively removed the distinction between hemp and marijuana in the U.S., outlawing the cultivation of hemp except where the DEA issues a limited-use permit—which they rarely do.

18. Before 1850, when a process for making pulp paper was introduced, most paper was made from hemp or cotton. Barkley Ogden, head of

UC-Berkeley's Library Conservation Department, said, "We've always had preservation problems in libraries and we've been able to do quite well in solving those problems. The problem with books printed since 1850 is different and overwhelming." (Source: "Libraries Face Big Loss of Aging 'Brittle Books,'" *Sacramento Bee* (Nov. 8, 1981), p. A22.) Hemp fiber contains the highest cellulose and lowest lignin content; much of the energy and chemical-intensive method for pulp processing is related to the removal of lignin. The use of hemp in paper products produces a stronger paper with the use of less-toxic processes. (Source: Erik Rothenberg, "A Renewal of Common Sense: The Case for Hemp in 21st Century America," Vote Hemp News Release (March 2001). http://www.votehemp.com/PDF/renewal.pdf [Nov. 2002].

19. In 1999, the DEA went after imported hemp products. Three years later, the Canadian company Kenex Ltd. filed a NAFTA Notice of Arbitration claiming $20 million in lost profits based on the DEA seizure of a hemp birdseed shipment. The DEA claimed the seizure of the bird- seed was based on an unwritten "Zero THC" policy. So far, the courts have confirmed that this product was legal according to U.S. law at the time of seizure. Sources: David P. West, "Hemp and Marijuana: Myths & Realities" (Wisconsin: North American Industrial Hemp Council, 1998), pp. 10-11; Adam Eidinger, "Hemp NAFTA Suit Begins Arbitra- tion Phase" (Washington, D.C.: Vote Hemp Press Release, Aug. 2, 2002). http://www.votehemp.com/PR/8-102_NAFTA_filed.html [Nov. 2002].

20. It is worth noting that in addition to the amount we spend on imported hemp, $9 million is spent annually by the DEA on the *Domestic Cannabis Eradication/Suppression Program* and antimarijuana task force. According to the *Vermont State Auditor's Report on The Domestic Eradica- tion Suppression Program* (1998), 99 percent of the cannabis destroyed was not marijuana, but feral, nonpsychoactive hemp. Source: Rothen- berg, "A Renewal of Common Sense," p. 20.

21. "By 1999, worldwide retail receipts were estimated at $150 million with the U.S. consumer purchasing over 60 percent of that amount. These numbers do not take into account the large quantities absorbed by com- mercial and industrial users in the U.S. and around the world, whose

major purchases have justified the planting of tens of thousands of acres in [hemp-cultivating] countries. . . . Ford's 1999–2000 use of hemp fiber was 5 million [pounds] and [was] expected to triple by 2002." Source: Rothenberg, "A Renewal of Common Sense," p. 9, 20.

22. In fiscal 1999, federal, state, and local governments spent over $146 billion for civil and criminal justice, an 8 percent increase over 1998. This amount includes estimates of government expenditures for the criminal justice functions of the national, state, and local governments, including: police protection, all judicial (including prosecution, courts, and public defense), and corrections. For every resident, the three levels of government together spent $521. (Source: U.S. DOJ, BJS, "Expenditure and Employment Statistics," 1999. http://www.ojp.usdoj.gov/bjs/eande.htm [Nov. 2002].) Total arrests in the United States in 2001 were 13,699,254. (Source: FBI Uniform Crime Reports, "Crime in the United States—2001," Table 29. http://www.fbi.gov/ucr/ 01cius.htm [Nov. 2002].) There were 723,627 marijuana arrests in 2001, or 5.3 percent of all arrests. Assuming that the rate of expenditure stayed at 1999 levels, 5.3 percent of $146 billion is $7.7 billion.

23. *The Shafer Report,* p. 657. These figures have changed by only a few percentage points over the past 20 years.

24. Summary of Findings from the 2000 National Household Survey on Drug Abuse, "Illicit Drug Use," http://www.samhsa.gov/oas/NHSDA/2kNHSDA/chapter2.htm [Nov. 2002].

25. Jack Curtin, professor in the criminal justice department at San Francisco State University in 1981, claimed that no "guesstimate" regarding time served in pretrial detention can be made because there are virtually no local statistics. Ron Bowens, sheriff's deputy in San Francisco, who worked in the pretrial detention center in 1981, claimed 90 days was average.

26. This is the average annual pay according to the U.S. Census Bureau,

"Statistical Abstract of the United States, 2001: U.S. Statistics in Brief," http://www.census.gov/statab/www/part3.html#employ [Nov. 2002].

27. Interview, October 22,1982.

28 Chuck Thomas, "Marijuana Arrests and Incarceration in the U.S."

29. NORML quoted "public funds incarcerating nonviolent marijuana offenders at a cost of $23,000 per year." (Source: Steven R. Donziger, ed., *The Real War on Crime: The Report of the National Criminal Justice Commission* (New York City: HarperPerennial, 1996).) MPP estimated the cost at "over $20,000 per prisoner for a total cost to taxpayers of marijuana related incarceration at $1.2 billion per year." (Source: Thomas, "Marijuana Arrests and Incarceration in the U.S.").

30. "From 1980 to 1999, the price tag for a public school education adjusted for inflation rose from roughly $5,000 to $8,000 per child, an increase of 60 percent." Source: Darcy A. Olsen, "The Department of Education: An Anti-Celebration," CATO Institute Report (May 4, 2000). http://www.cato.org/dailys/05-04-00.html [Nov. 2002].

31. U.S. DOJ, "Budget Trend Data from 1975 through the President's 2002 Request to Congress" (Summer 2001), p. 16. http://www.usdoj.gov/jmd/budgetsummary/btd/1975_2002/btd01 tocpg htm [Dec. 2002].

32. Costs of education from The National Center for Public Policy and Higher Education, "Losing Ground: A National Status Report on the Affordability of American Higher Education" (May 2002). http://www.highereducation.org/reports/losing_ground/ar9.shtml [Nov. 2002]. Prison costs are taken from NORML quoting Donziger, ed., *The Real War on Crime.*

33. Vince Schiraldi, "Spend more money on education not prisons," *Newsday* (Aug. 29, 2002). http://www.mapinc.org/newscecj/v02/n1620/a10.htm [Nov. 2002].

34. Chuck Thomas, "Marijuana Arrests and Incarceration in the U.S."

35. Ibid.

4 Health Effects

1. Ethan A. Nadelmann, "Should We Legalize Drugs? History Answers Yes," *American Heritage* (Feb./Mar. 1993), pp. 42-48.

2 Nalepka continues to back this viewpoint and is a vocal opponent of medical marijuana. The views she espouses can be assessed on her website, www.ourdrugfreekids.com.

3. Substance Abuse and Mental Health Services Administration (SAMHSA), Office of Applied Studies (OAS), "Marijuana Treatment Admissions Increase: 1993–1999," Drug Alcohol Services Information System (DASIS) Report (Jan. 18, 2002).
http://www.samhsa.gov/oas/2k2/MJtx.cfm [Nov. 2002].

4. A third of admissions for marijuana between 1993–1999 were ages 12–17; another third were ages 18–25. Source: Ibid.

5. Ibid.

6. Ibid.

7. "Marijuana Use and Drug Dependence," The National Household Survey on Drug Abuse (NHSDA) Report (Aug. 23, 2002).
http://www.samhsa.gov/oas/2k2/MJ&dependence/MJ&dependence. htm [Nov. 2002]. Also see p. 29-32 for other estimates of the number of marijuana users.

8. SAMHSA, OAS, Treatment Episode Data Sets (TEDS), *National Admissions to Substance Abuse Treatment Services 1994–1999* (DASIS Series S-14), Table 5.6.

9. Ibid.

10. National Institute on Drug Abuse (NIDA) Statistical Series Annual Data, 1981. Data from the Client Oriented Data Acquisition Process (Series E #25), NIDA Division of Data and Information Development (Sept. 1982), Table 20.

11. Interview with G.X., January 18, 1983.

12. SAMHSA, OAS, "Emergency Department Trends from the Drug Abuse Warning Network (DAWN), Preliminary Estimates January-June 2001, with Revised Estimates 1994-2000," (Feb. 2002), pp. 18, 40. http://www.samhsa.gov/oas/dawn/TrndED/2001/Text/TrndEDtxt. PDF [Nov. 2002].

13. Ibid, p. 22.

14. "SAMHSA Releases 2001 DAWN Survey," SAMHSA Press Release (Aug. 21, 2001). http://www.jointogether.org/sa/news/alerts/reader/0,1854,553494,00. html [Nov. 2002].

15. SAMHSA, OAS, "Emergency Department Trends from DAWN," p. 40.

16. Ibid, p. 22.

17. "An exhaustive search of the literature finds no deaths induced by marijuana. DAWN records instances of drug mentions in medical examiners' reports, and though marijuana is mentioned, it is usually in combination with alcohol or other drugs. Marijuana alone has not been shown to cause an overdose death. "Media Awareness Project (MAP Inc.), "Drug War Facts: Annual Causes of Death in the United States" (Sept. 8, 2001). http://www.drugwarfacts.org/causes.htm [Nov. 2002].

18. T. H. Mikuriya, "Historical Aspects of Cannabis Sativa in Western Medicine," *New Physician* (1969), p. 905.

19. Ibid. pp. 227-228.

20. F. S Stinson, T. M. Nephew, M. C. Dufour, and B. F. Grant, "State Trends in Alcohol-Related Mortality, 1979-1992," *U. S. Alcohol Epidemiologic Data Reference Manual*, vol. 5 (Washington, D.C.: U.S. GPO, National Institute on Alcohol Abuse and Alcoholism [NIAAA], 1996). http://www.niaaa.nih.gov/publications/sarm7992.txt [Oct. 2002].

21. The 1997 Centers for Disease Control report was cited by Common Sense for Drug Policy in "Annual Causes of Death in the United States" (March 2001), www.csdp.org/ads/causes.html [Oct. 2002].

22. NIAAA, "Number of deaths and age-adjusted death rates per 100,000 population for categories of alcohol-related mortality, United States and States, 1979–96" (Aug. 2001). http://www.niaaa.nih.gov/databases/armort01.txt [Dec 2002].

23. Common Sense for Drug Policy, "Annual Causes of Death in the United States."

24. *Annals of Internal Medicine* (Sept. 15, 1997), cited by Common Sense for Drug Policy in "Annual Causes of Death in the U.S."

25. SAMHSA, OAS, *Mortality Data from the Drug Abuse Warning Network 2000*, DAWN Series D-19, DHHS Publication No. (SMA) 02-3633, (Feb. 2002). http://www.samhsa.gov/oas/DAWN/mortality2k.pdf [Dec. 2002].

26. Ibid.

27. J. Lazarou, B. H. Pomeranz, and P. N. Corey, "Incidence of adverse drug reactions in hospitalized patients: a meta-analysis of prospective studies," *Journal of the American Medical Association* (Chicago, IL: American Medical Association, 1998) cited by Common Sense for Drug Policy in "Annual Causes of Death in the U.S."

28. Janet E. Joy, Stanley J. Watson, Jr., and John A. Benson, Jr., "Marijuana and Medicine: Assessing the Science Base," Division of Neuroscience and Behavioral Research, Institute of Medicine (Washington, D.C.: National Academy Press, 1999).

http://www.nap.edu/html/marimed/ [Oct. 2002]; and U.S. DOJ, DEA, "In the Matter of Marijuana Rescheduling Petition," Docket #86-22 (Sept. 6, 1988), p. 57, cited by Common Sense for Drug Policy in "Annual Causes of Death in the U.S."

29. Action on Smoking and Health, "Tobacco Deaths Overwhelm Other Causes" (June 2001).
http://www.no-smoking.org/june01/06-28-01-4.html [Nov. 2002], taken from Centers for Disease Control, National Center for Health Statistics (NCHS), "National Vital Statistics Reports for 1999."

30. Hindrik Robbe and James O'Hanion, "Marijuana and Actual Driving Performance," published as a Department of Transportation Report, #DOT HS 808-078 (1996).

31. NORML Foundation, "Marijuana and Driving: A Review of the Scientific Evidence," NORML News Release (Oct. 2002).
http://www.norml.org/index.cfm?Group_ID=5450 [Nov. 2002].

5 Hemp: Industrial Applications

1. The Hemp Industries Association (HIA), "US Legislation" (March 2001).
http://www.thehia.org/legislation.htm [Oct. 2002].

2. When hemp was outlawed, bird breeders complained that they couldn't breed their birds without hemp seeds and were allowed to use sterile hemp seeds instead.

3. Almost half of the agricultural chemicals used on U.S. crops are applied to cotton. Source: HIA, "Hemp Facts,"
http://www.thehia.org/hempfacts.htm [Nov. 2002].

4. Excerpted from Woody Harrelson's public statement at the time of his arrest, 1996.

5. Udo Erasmus, Ph.D., *Fats that Kill, Fats that Heal* (Alive Books, 1995).

6. Jay Kirschenbaum, "Would Hemp Help Farms?" *Argus Leader* (Oct. 27, 2002), cited from global hemp web site: http://www.globalhemp.com/News/2002/October/ would_hemp_help_farms.shtml [Nov. 2002].

7. "State Hemp Legislation," Vote Hemp Press Release (2001). http://www.votehemp.com/issue.html#Common [Nov. 2002].

8. HIA, "U.S. Legislation."

9. Don Lipton and Mace Thornton, "Alternative Crops Under Development," 1998 Virtual Convention (Charlotte, N.C., Jan. 12, 1998). http://www.fb.org/annual/amnews/nr/nr0103.html [Nov. 2002].

10. "Industrial Hemp and Other Alternative Crops for Small-Scale Tobacco Producers," USDA Agricultural Research Service and Economic Research Service for Karl Stauber, Under Secretary for Research, Education, and Economics. Published by USDA in 1995.

11. Adam Eidinger, "Hemp NAFTA Suit Begins Arbitration Phase," Vote Hemp Press Release (Aug. 2, 2002). http://www.votehemp.com/PR/8-102_NAFTA_filed.html [Nov. 2002].

6 Medical Applications

1. U.S. DOJ, DEA, "In the Matter of Marijuana Rescheduling Petition, Opinion and Recommended Ruling, Findings of Fact, Conclusions of Law and Decision of Administrative Law Judge Francis L. Young, Part VIII: Accepted Safety for Use under Medical Supervision," Docket No. 86-22 (Sept. 8, 1988).

2. Martin Martinez, *The New Prescription: Marijuana as Medicine* (California: Quick American Archives, 2000), pp. 23-25.

3. P. Tashkin, B. J. Shapiro, Y. E. Lee, and C. B. Harper, "Effects of Smoked Marihuana and Experimentally Induced Asthma," *American Review of Respiratory Diseases* 112 (1975), pp. 377-86.

4. Formukong, Evans, and Evans, "Analgesic and anti-inflammatory activity of constituents of cannabis sativa L.," *Inflammation* 12:4 (1988), pp. 361-71.

5. Vincent Vinciguerra, M.D., Terry Moore, MSW, and Eileen Brennan, RN, "Inhalation Marijuana as an Anti-emetic for Cancer Chemotherapy," *New York State Journal of Medicine* 85 (1988), pp. 525-27; D. Dansac, "In the Matter of Marijuana Rescheduling Petition," affidavit filed in DEA hearings, Docket 86-22 (1987).

6. Beltramo and Piomelli, "Functional role of high-affinity anandamide transport, as revealed by selective inhibition," *Science* 277:5329 (1997), p. 1094(4); Formukong, Evans, and Evans, "Analgesic and anti-inflammatory activity of constituents of cannabis sativa L."

7. Lester Grinspoon and James B. Bakalar, *Marihuana: The Forbidden Medicine* (Connecticut: Yale University Press, 1997), pp. 115-17.

8. Martin Martinez, *The New Prescription: Marijuana as Medicine* (California: Quick American Archives, 2000), pp. 62-63.

9. R. S. Hepler and I. R. Frank, "Marijuana Smoking and Intraocular Pressure," *Journal of the American Medical Association* 217 (1971), p. 1392; Franjo Grotenhermen, M.D., "Review of Therapeutic Effects," in *Cannabis and Cannabinoids*, Grotenhermen and Ethan Russo, M.D., eds. (New York: Haworth Press, 2002), p. 129.

10. Grinspoon and Bakalar, *Marihuana: The Forbidden Medicine*, pp. 113-14.

11. P. A. Fried, "Postnatal Consequences of Maternal Marijuana Use," in T. M. Pinkert, ed., *Current Research on the Consequences of Maternal Drug Abuse* (Rockville, MD: National Institute on Drug Abuse), pp. 61-72; P. A. Fried and B. Watkinson, "12- and 24-Month Neurobehavioral Follow-Up of Children Prenatally Exposed to Marijuana, Cigarettes and Alcohol," *Neurotoxicology and Teratology* 10 (1988), pp. 305-13.

12. W. Notcutt, M. Price, S. Newport, C. Sansom, and S. Simmons, "Medicinal Cannabis Extract in Chronic Pain: Design of a Comparative 'N of 1'

Primary Study," and "Results from Long-Term Safety Extension Study," presented at the International Cannabinoid Research Society meetings (Monterey, California, June 2002).

13. National Multiple Sclerosis Society website. http://www.nationalmssociety.org [Nov. 2002].

14. D. J. Petro, "Marijuana as a Therapeutic Agent for Muscle Spasm or Spasticity," *Psychosomatics* 21 (1980), pp. 81-85; Richard E. Musty and Paul Consroe, "Spastic Disorders," in *Cannabis and Cannabinoids,* Grotenhermen and Russo, eds. (New York: Haworth Press, 2002), pp. 129, 196.

15 Ethan Russo, "Migraine," in *Cannabis and Cannabinoids,* Grotenhermen and Russo, eds. (New York: Haworth Press, 2002), pp. 129, 187-93.

16. J. Malec, R. F. Harvey, and J. J. Cayner, "Cannabis Effect on Spasticity in Spinal Cord Injury," *Archives of Physical and Medical Rehabilitation* 63 (March 1982), pp. 116-18.

17. Franjo Grotenhermen M.D., "Review of Therapeutic Effects," in *Cannabis and Cannabinoids,* Grotenhermen and Russo, eds. (New York: Haworth Press, 2002), p. 130.

18. B. A. Carlini and J. M. Cunha, "Hypnotic and Antiepileptic Effects of Cannabidiol," *Journal of Clinical Pharmacology* 21 (1981), pp. 417S-427S.

19. "Petition to Repeal Marijuana Prohibition Filed By Jon Gettman," *Activist News.* (Nov. 1995). http://www.ndsn.org/NOV95/PETITION.html [Nov. 2002].

20. Schedule III drugs, by contrast, have a lower potential for abuse than either Schedule I or II drugs, and also have an accepted medical use. These include codeine, aspirin, and some barbiturates. Schedule IV drugs, such as Valium and Xanax, are believed to have a very low potential for abuse and a medical use. Drugs in the last category, Schedule V, are still said to "have a potential for limited physical or psychological dependence," and include over-the-counter cough

medicines. Source: U.S. DOJ, DEA, *Controlled Substances Act of 1970,* Title 21, Chapter 13, Section 812.

21. Janet E. Joy, Stanley J. Watson, Jr., and John A. Benson, Jr., eds., *Marijuana and Medicine: Assessing the Science Base,* Institute of Medicine, National Academy of Sciences (1999).

22. Ibid.

23. Personal communication, 1996.

24. CNN special, "Higher Times," 1997.

25. Several patients made this point to the author during a visit to the San Francisco Cannabis Buyers' Club, 1996.

26. In recent studies of marijuana's effectiveness for multiple sclerosis, THC by itself, as it is in Marinol, has been found to be ineffective for pain relief. The most efficacious formula contained a combination of CBD and THC. No synthetic cannabis-based medicine currently offers this combination. Source: Notcutt, et al., "Medicinal Cannabis Extract in Chronic Pain" and "Results from Long-Term Safety Extension Study."

27. Personal communication, 1996.

28. S. Agurell, et al., "Pharmacokinetics and Metabolism of Delta-1-Tetrahydrocannabinol and Other Cannabinoids with Emphasis on Man," *Pharmacological Reviews* 38 (1986), pp. 21-43.

29. Notcutt, et al., "Medicinal Cannabis Extract in Chronic Pain" and "Results from Long-Term Safety Extension Study."

30. Personal communication, 1996.

31. Dale Gieringer, published response to editorial in the *San Diego Union Tribune,* June 12, 1996. Studies conducted to explore marijuana's therapeutic effects in the late 1970s include S. Cohen, "Therapeutic Aspects,"

in R. C. Petersen, ed., *Marijuana Research Findings, 1976* (Rockville, MD: NIDA, 1977), pp. 194-225; S. Cohen and R. C. Stillman, eds., *The Therapeutic Potential of Marijuana* (New York: Plenum, 1976); NIDA, Marijuana and Health Report to Congress (1980).

32. Dr. Donald Abrams, a neurologist who works with AIDS patients at San Francisco General Hospital, had received grants for previous research. He applied to do research on the use of cannabis to treat AIDS symptoms, but his protocols were repeatedly rejected by the NIDA. He was allowed to conduct a study to see whether marijuana was harmful to AIDS patients. A letter he wrote to NIDA expressed his frustrations with their inflexible policy regarding marijuana studies. Source: Letter from Donald Abrams to Alan Leshner, April 1995.
http://www.maps.org/mmj/abrams.html [Nov. 2002].

33. "Favorable medical marijuana laws have been enacted in 35 states since 1978. However, most of these laws are ineffectual, due to the federal government's overarching prohibition. (Five of these laws have since expired or been repealed.) Currently, 30 states and the District of Columbia have laws on the books that recognize marijuana's medical value: Twelve states with 'Therapeutic Research Program' laws are nevertheless unable to give patients legal access to medical marijuana because of federal obstructionism; ten states and the District of Columbia have symbolic laws that recognize marijuana's medical value but fail to provide patients with protection from arrest. And, since 1996, eight states have enacted laws that effectively allow patients to use medical marijuana despite federal law." Source: Richard Schmitz and Chuck Thomas, "State-By-State Medical Marijuana Laws," MPP News Release (June 2001).
http://www.mpp.org/ statelaw/index.html [Nov. 2002].

34. R. Doblin and M. A. R. Kleiman, "Marijuana as an Anti-Emetic Medicine: A Survey of Oncologists' Attitudes and Experiences," *Journal of Clinical Oncology* 19 (1991), pp. 1275-90.

35. A. B. Chang, et al., "Delta-Nine-Tetrahydrocannabinol as an Antiemetic in Cancer Patients Receiving High-Dose Methotrexate: A Prospective Randomized Evaluation" *Annals of Internal Medicine* 91 (1979), pp. 819-24.

36. Vinciguerra, et al., "Inhalation Marijuana as an Anti-emetic for Cancer Chemotherapy."

37. Donald Abrams' research findings for the study "Short Term Effects of Cannabinoids in HIV Patients" were reported at the 13th International AIDS conference in Durban, South Africa, July 13, 2000. A summary of this presentation appears on the Cannabis MD web site: http://www.cannabismd.com/reports/abrams1.php [Nov. 2002].

38. Andrew Weil, M.D., "Therapeutic Hemp Oil," http://www.ratical.org/renewables/TherapHoil.html [Nov. 2002].

39. Ibid.

40. Udo Erasmus, *Fats That Heal, Fats That Kill*, p. 268.

41. Ibid, p. 399.

42. Ibid, p. 236.

43. Ibid, p. 275.

7 National Security

1. U.S. DOJ, DEA, National Narcotics Intelligence Consumers Committee 1995, "The Supply of Illicit Drugs to the United States" (Aug. 1996). http://www.fas.org/irp/agency/doj/dea/product/nnicc-95.htm [Nov. 2002].

2. Ibid.

3. U.S. DOJ, DEA, "Drug Intelligence Brief: The Cannabis Situation in the United States." (Dec. 1999). http://www.usdoj.gov/dea/pubs/intel/99028/99028.html [Nov. 2002]; U.S. DOJ, DEA, "BC Bud: Growth of the Canadian Marijuana Trade," (December 2000). http://www.usdoj.gov/dea/pubs/intel/01001-intellbrief.pdf [Nov. 2002].

4. David Taylor, M.D., "Salmonellosis Associated with Marijuana," *New England Journal of Medicine* 306 (1982), pp. 1249-53.

5. J. M. McPartland, "Microbiological Contaminants of Marijuana," *Journal of the International Hemp Association* 1 (1994), pp. 41-44. http://www.hempfood.com/IHA/iha01205.html [Nov. 2002].

6. U.S. DOJ, DEA, "The Cannabis Situation in the U.S."

7. Ibid.

8. Transnational Institute, "Breaking the Impasse: Polarisation & Paralysis in UN Drug Control," Drugs and Conflict Debate Paper, no. 5 (July 2002). http://www.tni.org/reports/drugs/ debate5.htm [Nov. 2002].

9. A complete description and analysis of Operation Intercept is recorded in Brecher, *Licit & Illicit Drugs*, p. 434.

10. In a recent trip to Vancouver, Czar Walters implied that he would tighten the U.S.-Canada border in order to curtail marijuana smuggling. He claimed to quote Canadian Police Force information, stating that 95 percent of Canadian-grown marijuana is imported to the U.S. Where he got this erroneous figure is unclear, but U.S. figures show that only 1 metric ton was seized along the border in 2000. Source: Robert Matas, "U.S. Drug Chief Warns against Injection Sites for Addicts," *Globe and Mail*, (Vancouver, BC, Nov. 21, 2002).
http://www.mapinc.org/drugnews/ v02/n2130/a05.html?397 [Nov. 2002].

11. U.S. DOJ, BJS, "Intelligence Brief: National Drug Threat Assessment" (Aug. 2002). http://www.usdoj.gov/ndic/pubs/1335/index.htm [Nov. 2002].

12. ONDCP, "What America's Drug Users Spend on Illegal Drugs 1988-1998" (Dec. 2000), http.www.whitehousedrugpolicy.gov/publications/ drugfact/American_users_spend.html [Nov. 2002].

13. The NAFTA Office of Mexico in Canada, "Mexico's Integration to the Global Economy" (2002).
http://www.nafta-mexico.org/trade/Mexico_s_trade/mexico_s_trade.html [Nov. 2002].

14. Pete Brady, "Jamaica's Ganja Study," *Cannabis Culture* 37 (Aug. 2002) pp. 54-57.

15. "Ganja in Jamaica: Commission Urges Legalization," About.com website, http://substanceabuse.miningco.com/library/weekly/aa090101.htm [Nov. 2002].

16. Ibid.

17. Pete Brady, "Jamaica's Ganja Study."

18. Reuters Wire, "Jamaican Parliament to Debate Marijuana Status" (Feb. 12, 2002).
http://www.mapinc.org/drugnews/v02/n239/a01.html?1193 [Nov. 2002].

19. NORML Foundation, "Jamaica Parliament Ponders Marijuana Decriminalization," NORML Foundation News Release (Feb. 14, 2002).

20. David Williams, "US threatens Jamaica over ganja," *Jamaica Gleaner* (May 21, 2002).
http://www.jamaica-gleaner.com/gleaner/20010817/lead/lead1.html [Nov. 2002].

21. Ibid.

22. Ibid.

23. Ira Teinowitz, "White House Brings Back Ads Linking Drugs to Terrorism," *AdAge.com* magazine (Sept. 17, 2002).
http://www.adage.com/news.cms?newsId=36048 [Nov. 2002].

24. Naftali Bendavid, "Linking drug money to terrorism may backfire," *The Macon Telegraph* (March 22, 2002).
http://www.macon.com/mld/macon/news/nation/2916659.htm [Nov. 2002].

25. Ibid.

26. Bill Berkowitz, "DEA Launches Exhibit Proclaiming Drugs = Terrorism," *TomPaine.common sense* online public-interest journal (Aug. 28, 2002).
http://www.tompaine.com/feature.cfm/ ID/6258 [Nov. 2002].

27. "Iraq's oil exports under a UN humanitarian programme were running at around one million barrels per day (bpd), or under half the normal rate of 2.2 million bpd. US refiners are buying the overwhelming majority of Iraqi oil exports through small companies and traders." Thus an SUV contributes more to terrorism than smoking a joint. Source: Agence France-Presse, "U.S. refiners buying overwhelming majority of Iraqi oil exports" (Feb. 2001).
http://www.casi.org.uk/discuss/2001/msg00125.html [Nov. 2002].

28. Ibid.

29. NORML Foundation, "Zogby Poll: majority of Americans Oppose US Marijuana Policies," NORML Press Release (Dec. 6, 2001).
http:www.norml.org/index.cfm?Group_ID=4383 [Dec. 2002].

8 Sociological Aspects

1. Ethan Nadelmann and Jann Wenner, "Toward a Sane National Drug Policy," *Rolling Stone* (May, 5, 1994), pp. 24-26.

2. "The American Bar Association . . . concurs in the view that marijuana laws that criminalize the millions of Americans who have used marijuana engender disrespect for the law." Source: NAS, National Research Council (NRC), "An Analysis of Marijuana Policy" (1982), p. 16.

http://www.druglibrary.org/schaffer/Library/studies/nas/back.htm [Nov. 2002].

3. Ibid.

4. Ibid. p. 15.

5. Ibid. According to a 2002 NORML report, "Marijuana smokers in this country are no different from their nonsmoking peers, except for their marijuana use.... They are otherwise law-abiding citizens who live in fear of arrest and imprisonment solely because they choose to smoke marijuana for relaxation instead of drinking alcohol. Marijuana prohibition is a misapplication of the criminal sanction which undermines respect for the law in general and extends government into inappropriate areas of private lives." Source: NORML Foundation, "Sixty Years of Marijuana Prohibition in the U.S."

6. NORML Foundation, "'Misinterpreted' Drug Law Denies 87,000 Students their Financial Aid," NORML Press Release (Sept. 12, 2002). http://www.norml.org/index.cfm?Group_ID=5412 [Dec. 2002].

7. Kevin Nelson, "2001: A Year in the Life of Marijuana Prohibition," Alternet.org (Jan. 7, 2002). http://www.alternet.org/story. html?StoryID=12172 [Nov. 2002].

8. Joseph Roundtree Foundation, "Young People and Drugs," *Social Policy Research* 133 (Nov. 1997). http://www.jrf.org.uk/knowledge/findings/socialpolicy/sp133.asp [Nov. 2002].

9. Ibid.

10. Personal communication, 1983. Since that time other people have told me of similar feelings and attitudes toward the marijuana laws and their enforcement.

11. Edvins Beitkis, "A New Breed of Marijuana Farmer," *San Francisco Chronicle/Examiner* (July 18, 1982), p. B1.

12. Sharon Bibb, "Americans Are Casual but Ambivalent About Pot," *Oakland Tribune* (March 12, 1982), p. D1.

13. "Forfeiture provisions authoriz[e] law enforcement agencies to seize 'drug-related' assets, like a house in which marijuana plants have been grown, and use the proceeds for their budgetary needs. . . . [such] programs have distorted governmental policy-making and law enforcement. During the past decade, law enforcement agencies have turned to asset seizures and drug enforcement grants to compensate for budgetary shortfalls, at the expense of other criminal justice goals. We believe the strange shape of the criminal justice system today . . . is largely the unplanned byproduct of this economic incentive structure." Source: Eric Blumenson and Eva Nilsen, "Policing for Profit: The Drug War's Hidden Economic Agenda," *University of Chicago Law Review* (1997).
http://www.fear.org/menuidx2.html [Dec. 2002].

14. Interview with Tim L., Dec. 7, 1982.

15. According to London newspaper *The Guardian,* "Despite the arrest rate, cannabis possession is regarded by many senior police officers to be a trivial offence—nevertheless it consumes an estimated 74,000 man hours a year in London alone. The proposals are intended to free up police time to concentrate on more serious crimes and harder drugs." Source: Simon Jeffery, "Reclassifying Cannabis," *Guardian* Unlimited Special Report (London, Oct. 25, 2001).
http://www.guardian.co.uk/drugs/Story/0,2763,580507,00.html [Dec. 2002].

16. "The home secretary told MPs yesterday that the changes would not detract from the simple message that all drugs were harmful but it would make a clearer distinction between cannabis and class A drugs such as heroin and cocaine. . . . In spite of focusing on hard drugs, the majority of police time is currently spent on handling cannabis offences. It is time

for an honest and commonsense approach focusing effectively on drugs that cause the most harm." Source: Alan Travis, "Cannabis Laws Eased in Drug Policy Shakeup," *The Guardian* (London, Oct. 24, 2001). http://www.guardian.co.uk/drugs/Story/0,2763,579901,00.html [Dec. 2002].

17. "Canadian Senate Panel Urges Legalization of Pot," CNN.com online news report (Sept. 4, 2002). http://www.cnn.com/2002/WORLD/americas/09/04/canada.pot/ [Dec. 2002].

18. Interview with Dr. Jerome Skolnik, Nov. 8, 1982. Reports on driving while black and drug-arrest statistics lead to the conclusion that minorities are far more likely to be arrested for drug use at racially motivated police discretion.

19. NORML Foundation, "Sixty Years of Marijuana Prohibition in the U.S."

20. U.S. DOJ, BJS, "Federal Drug Offenders, 1999 with Trends 1984-99," NCJ 187285 (Aug. 2001), p. 11.

21. NORML Foundation, "Sixty Years of Marijuana Prohibition in the U.S."

22. Michael R. Aldrich, "A Brief Legal History of Marijuana," Do It Now Foundation pamphlet, n.d., p. 14.

23. David F. Musto, M.D., "The Marijuana Tax Act of 1937," *Archives of General Psychiatry* 26 (Feb. 1972), p. 101.

24. Ibid, p. 104.

25. NAS, NRC, "An Analysis of Marijuana Policy," p. 2.

26. Texas DARE Institute, 2000. http://147.26.206.16/dare/Info/Texas_DARE_DARE_History_Info. htm [Dec. 2002].

27. Drug Reform Coordination Network (DRCNet) "A Different Look at DARE: How Much Money Is Spent on DARE" (1995). http://www.drcnet.org/DARE/daremoney.html#moneyspent [Dec. 2002].

28. Children in DARE programs are asked to indicate the names of people they could tell if "a friend finds some pills" or they "are asked to keep a secret." In such materials, police officers are always listed as people to whom children should report suspicious activity.

29. Susan Ennett, et al., "How Effective Is Drug Abuse Resistance Education: A Meta-Analysis of DARE," *American Journal of Public Health*, Sept. 84: 9 (1994), p. 1399.

30. "Makes No Difference If Kids DARE," *Education Reporter* #164 (Sept. 1999). http://www.eagleforum.org/educate/1999/sept99/dare. html [Dec. 2002].

31. Ibid.

32. Ibid.

33. DRCNet, "A Different Look at DARE: What's Wrong with DARE," section 6, 1995. http://www.drcnet.org/DARE/section6.html [Dec. 2002].

34. DRCNet, "A Different Look at DARE: How Much Money Is Spent on DARE."

35. "Currently there are approximately 6.6 million people in the U.S. correctional system. This means that one of every 32 adults is either behind bars or on probation." Source: The Witherspoon Society, "Washington Office reports on rising prison populations even as crime rates fall" (Oct. 2002). http://www.witherspoonsociety.org/criminal_justice.htm [Dec. 2002].

36. U.S. DOJ, DEA, "In the Matter of Marijuana Rescheduling Petition," Judge Young.

9 Why Marijuana Isn't Legal

1. FBI Uniform Crime Reports, "Crime in the United States—2000," Section IV, p. 216, Tables 4.1 and 29; California NORML, "Marijuana Violations for Year 2000 Hit All Time High."

2. The government records the number of arrests, not the number of people arrested. Therefore, 14 million arrests does not mean that 14 million people were arrested, since some people were arrested more than once during the year. FBI Uniform Crime Reports, "Crime in the United States—2000," Section IV, p. 215.

3. U.S. DOJ, BJS, "Prison and Jail Inmates at Mid-Year 2001," NCJ 191702 (Apr. 2002).
http://www.ojp.usdoj.gov/bjs/pub/pdf/pjim01.pdf [Dec. 2002].

4. Based on 1997 figures, policy analyst Chuck Thomas estimated that 40,000 of the 1,134,723 prisoners were serving time in state and federal prisons for marijuana charges. If we extrapolate these figures to the same 4 percent of the 2 million prisoners currently serving time, an estimated 80,000 people are in jail or prison for marijuana. Source: Thomas, "Marijuana Arrests and Incarceration in the U.S."

5. U.S. DOJ, BJS, "Federal Drug Offenders 1999, with Trends 1984-99," NCJ 187285, p. 9; U.S. DOJ, BJS, Prisoners in 1999; Prisoners in 2000; Prisoners in 2001.

6. "During the 1990s, corrections constituted one of the fastest growing line items in state budgets. On average, corrections consumed 7 percent of state budgets in 2000. Today, it is costing states, counties and federal government nearly $40 billion to imprison approximately two million state and local inmates, up from $5 billion in combined prison and jail expenditures in 1978." Source: Judith Greene and Vincent Schiraldi, *Cutting Correctly: New Prison Policies for Times of Fiscal Crisis* (Feb. 7, 2002).
http://www.justicepolicy.org/cutting/cutting_main.html [Dec. 2002].

7. For information on this figure, see the box, "How many people use marijuana" in chapter 3, pp. 29-32.

8. FBI Uniform Crime Reports, "Crime in the United States—2000," Section IV, p. 216, Tables 4.1 and 29; California NORML, "Marijuana Violations for Year 2000 Hit All Time High."

9. According to the BJS, "In fiscal 1999, federal, state, and local governments spent over $146 billion for civil and criminal justice, an 8 percent increase over 1998." If we consider the increase since the 1999 statistics at a modest 4 percent per year, the expenditure for 2002 would be approximately $164 billion. Source: U.S. DOJ, BJS, "Expenditure and Employment Statistics: Summary Findings,"
http://www.ojp.usdoj.gov/bjs/eande.htm#selected [Dec. 2002].

10. In 2000, there were 1,579,566 state and local arrests for drug-abuse violations in the United States. Of these arrests, 5.6 percent were for marijuana sale/manufacturing, and 40.9 percent were for marijuana possession. Source: FBI Uniform Crime Reports, "Crime in the United States—2000," Section IV, p. 216, Tables 4.1 and 29.

11. DEA, "DEA Staffing and Budget" (2002).
http://www.dea.gov/ agency/staffing.htm [Dec. 2002].

12. For more information on Proposition 36, including the full text of the bill, see the California Proposition 36 website at www.prop36.org.

13. The California Online Voter Guide 2000, a project of the California Voter Foundation, presented both sides of the proposition and also listed the top financial donors for and against Prop. 36. While the pro-Prop. 36 raised ten times as much as its opponents, the main contributors in opposition were Police Associations, the California Sheriff's Association and the California District Attorney Associations. The Drug Free America Foundation was also listed among the top contributors. Those who signed "No" on the ballot arguments included the president of the California Association of Drug Court Professionals and the president of the Chief Probation Officers of California. Source: California Online Voter Guide 2000, "Proposition 36."
www.calvoter.org/2000/ general/propositions/36.html [Dec. 2002].

14. Drug Policy Alliance, "Proposition 36 One-Year Progress Report" (July 2002).
    http://www.prop36.org/one_year_report.html [Dec. 2002]; Gerald Uelman et al., "Substance Abuse and Crime Prevention Act of 2000: Progress Report." (March 2002).
    http://www.prop36.org/progress_report.html [Dec. 2002].

15. This list is excerpted directly from Elizabeth G. Hill, legislative analyst, "Implementing Proposition 36: Issues, Challenges, and Opportunities" (Dec. 14, 2000), figure 1, p. 2.
    http://www.lao.ca.gov/2000_reports/prop36/121400_prop_36.pdf [Dec. 2002].

16. California Online Voter Guide 2000, "Proposition 36."
    www.calvoter.org/2000/general/propositions/36.html [Dec. 2002].

17. John P. Walters, "The Myth of 'Harmless' Marijuana," *The Washington Post* (May 1, 2002).
    http://www.drugwatch.org/Walters%20marijuana%20myth.htm [Dec. 2002].

18. Dr. Tod Mikuriya, a physician and well-read author on the history of medical marijuana, states: "As chemical technology advanced, pharmaceutical preparations became more purified . . . with cannabin, cannabindon, cannabine and cannabinon being marketed by Merck in 1896. Cannabis was also combined with different drugs in proprietary preparations. For example, Squibb around the turn of the century included cannabis in 'Chlorodyne,' a gastrointestinal antispasmodic employing morphine as its main ingredient. . . . Because of the fluctuation of prices of Indian cannabis due to taxation policies of the British colonial government there were continuing efforts to develop American medicinal strains. From 1918 to 1937, Parke-Davis and Eli Lilly ran a joint research project at Parkedale, a botanical experimental facility near Rochester, Michigan in an effort to produce a viable American strain." Source: Tod Mikuriya, M.D., "Cannabis in Western Medicine: An Abbreviated History," *Journal of Psychedelic Drugs* 10:3 (July-Sept. 1978).
    http://www.mikuriya.com/canwest.html [Dec. 2002].

19. Jack Herer, "Cannabis Drug Use in the 19th Century," in *The Emperor Wears No Clothes*, 11th edition (1998), p. 83.
http://www.electricemperor.com/eecdrom/TEXT/TXTCH12.HTM
[Dec. 2002].

20. Herer notes in "Cannabis Drug Use" that "during all this time (until the 1940s), science, doctors, and drug manufacturers (Lilly, Parke-Davis, Squibb, etc.) had no idea of [marijuana's] active ingredients," p. 83. Professor Raphael Mechoulam discovered THC, the primary psychoactive component of marijuana, in 1964. Mechoulam has authored two books on the subject of his research. For more information on Mechoulam see David Pate's "Interview with Raphael Mechoulam," June 1994.
http://www.hempfood.com/IHA/iha01113.html [Dec. 2002].

21. Sources say that willow tree bark, containing the primary ingredient of aspirin, salicylic acid, was first documented by Hippocrates in the 5th century BC. The term "aspirin" originated in 1899, when a method was developed to commercially isolate and synthesize the primary ingredient of the plant in the less harsh form of acetylsalicylic acid. Although it is debated, this development is credited to Felix Hoffman and Heinrich Dreser, who both worked for Bayer at the time. Sources: "The History of Medicine: 1866-1900" Medhelpnet.com (2000).
http://www.medhelpnet.com/medhist6.html [Dec. 2002]; Anne Adina Judith Andermann, "Phycisians, Fads, and Pharmaceuticals: A History of Aspirin," McGill University paper (1996).
http://www.mjm.mcgill.ca/issues/v02n02/aspirin.html [Dec. 2002].

22. Mikuriya, "Cannabis in Western Medicine: An Abbreviated History."

23 "In Memory, Robert Randall, Father of the Medical Marijuana Movement," November Coalition (fall 2001).
http://www.november.org/razorwire/july-aug-sept2001/page35.html
[Dec. 2002].

24. Sheryl Gay Stolberg, "For a Very Few Patients, U.S. Provides Free Marijuana," *New York Times* (March 19, 1999).
http://www.marijuana.org/NYTimes3-19-99.html [Dec. 2002].

25. Ibid.

26. The International Cannabinoid Research Society (ICRS) includes the most prominent cannabinoid researchers among its active members. The ICRS website can be found at www.cannabinoidsociety.org.

27. ICRS Symposium, Acapulco, Mexico, June 1999. The GW Pharmaceutical website can be accessed at www.gwpharm.com.

28. ICRS Symposium, Monterey, California, June 2002.

29. Daniel Lundgren, attorney general, "Medical Use of Marijuana. Initiative Statute: Summary" (1996).
http://vote96.ss.ca.gov/Vote96/html/BP/215.htm [Dec. 2002].

30. James P. Fox, Michael J. Meyers, and Sharon Rose, "Argument Against Proposition 215," as provided in the 1996 California Voter Ballot information.
http://vote96.ss.ca.gov/Vote96/html/BP/215noarg.htm [Dec. 2002].

31. Ibid.

32. Carol Miller, "Prop. 215—Post Election Medical Information," *Sonoma County Free Press* (Dec. 1, 1996).
http://www.sonomacountyfreepress.com/scrap/scrp.html [Dec. 2002].

33. Levin was later acquitted of all charges. He and his wife spent $95,000 defending themselves against allegations by the district attorney that they had too much marijuana for medical use. In 2000, the Levins filed a suit against Shasta County for $1 million in damages for wrongful arrest and mistreatment while in custody. Sources: California NORML, "Medical MJ Advances Despite Setbacks, Struggles," California NORML Reports, April 2002.
http://www.canorml.org/news/prop215reportapr00.html [Dec. 2002];
California NORML, "The Continuing Ordeal of Prop. 215 Patients," California NORML Report, (Dec.1999).
http://www.canorml.org/news/prop215casesdec99.html [Dec. 2002].

34. "In the words of the man who busted him, now retired Orange County district attorney Carl Ambrust, Chavez is a 'street drug dealer' who ran a 'sophisticated drug operation' and 'hid behind the law.' . . . In truth, Chavez's chief crime was that he believed in the goodwill of the law-enforcement community . . . if Chavez was a drug dealer, he was an inept one. In late 1996, just weeks after Prop. 215's passage, he spoke with Garden Grove city officials, announcing his intention to open the co-op. . . . He religiously advertised his efforts in the local media, expanding on his vision with any reporter who would listen." (Source: Nick Schou, "Man of the Year 1998: Marvin Chavez," *Orange County Weekly*, January 1999.) Chavez was convicted and given a 6-year sentence, which he appealed. His appeal is ongoing, and he is currently serving time in Vallejo, California. To write to Marvin Chavez or read updates on his case, visit the Americans for Safe Access website at www.safeaccessnow.org.

35. The People v. Myron Carlyle Mower, Supreme Court of California, S094490, Ct. App. 5 No. F030690, County of Tuolumne, Super. Ct. No. CR1995, July 18, 2002. This decision can be viewed on the American Alliance for Medical Cannabis (AAMC)website at http://www.letfreedomgrow.com/articles/mower_decision.htm [Dec. 2002].

36. Trippet based her brief on the constitutional argument that patients using medical marijuana with a doctor's recommendation have the same rights as any patient with prescription medicine. See Pebbles Trippet, "California Supreme Court Issues Principled Medical Marijuana Ruling," Source: Medical Marijuana Patients Union website, July 20, 2002. http://www.mmpu.org/news_calisupremes.html [Dec. 2002] for her commentary on the Mower decision.

37. Ibid.

38. Eric Schleuter, a rabid medical-marijuana prosecutor, discusses his new attitude regarding prosecuting medical-marijuana cases in the following article: William Ferchland, "Supreme Court Sends Victory to Marijuana Patients" *Tahoe Daily Tribune,* July 23, 2002. http://www.cannabisnews.com/news/thread13507.shtml [Dec. 2002].

39. Kenneth Howe, John Wildermuth, and Yumi Wilson, "Hallinan Declares Victory," *San Francisco Chronicle* (Dec. 23, 1999). http://sfgate.com/cgibin/article.cgi?file=/chronicle/archive/1999/12/23/MN5255.DTL [Dec. 2002].

40. Eileen Morris, "Duo Acquitted in Pot Growing Case," *Argus-Courier* (May 2, 2001). http://www.cannabisnews.com/news/thread9577.shtml [Dec. 2002].

41. Patrick Sullivan, "Mullins [sic] Out, School Spending In," *North Bay Bohemian* (March 7-13, 2002). http://www.metroactive.com/papers/sonoma/03.07.02/election-0210.html [Dec. 2002].

42. "In upsets, Humboldt and Sonoma voters tossed out their incumbent DA's for challengers with a more liberal line on medical marijuana. The victors, Steve Passalacqua in Sonoma and Paul Gallegos in Humboldt, had both appealed to Prop. 215 supporters. The incumbents, Mike Mullins [sic] in Sonoma and Terry Farmer in Humboldt, had both been appointees on the Attorney General's Task Force on Medical Marijuana, where they took a cautious, law enforcement line. . . . Humboldt Sheriff Dennis Lewis, a bane of pot supporters and civil libertarians, was [also] overwhelmingly defeated by challenger Gary Philp." Source: Drug Policy Forum of California, "Prop 215 Supporters Fare Well in March 5th California Primary," March 2002 California Primary Election Guide. http://www.drugsense.org/dpfca/elect2002res_mar.html [Dec. 2002].

43. A December 2001 Zogby poll commissioned by NORML reported: "Two-thirds (67 percent) of respondents oppose the use of federal law enforcement agencies to close dispensaries that supply medical marijuana to patients in California and other states that have legalized pot for medical use. Of those, a full one-half (50 percent) say they 'strongly oppose.'" In addition the poll gauged the more general question of imprisoning nonviolent marijuana offenders: "Sixty-one percent of respondents said that in light of the increased attention to the threat of terrorism since September 11, they oppose arresting and

jailing nonviolent marijuana smokers." Source: NORML Foundation, "Zogby Poll: Majority of Americans Oppose US Marijuana Policies. http://www.norml.org/index.cfm?Group_ID=4383 [Dec. 2002]. The poll and its results can be viewed on the NORML website: www.norml.org.

44. As of 2002, Alaska, Arizona, California, Colorado, Hawaii, Maine, Nevada, Oregon, and Washington have enacted marijuana laws. See Richard Schmitz and Chuck Thomas, "State by State Medical Marijuana Laws, Marijuana Policy Project (MPP) Report" (June 2001). http://www.mpp.org/statelaw/ [Dec. 2002] for a comprehensive report on the history and development of state medical marijuana laws. Another source for up-to-date marijuana law by state is the NORML website at www.norml.org.

45. "In 1976, the Dutch adopted a formal written policy of nonenforcement for violations involving possession or sale of up to thirty grams [about an ounce] of cannabis. . . . In late 1995, this threshold was lowered to five grams in response to domestic and international pressures." Source: Robert J. MacCoun and Peter Reuter, *Drug War Heresies* (Cambridge: Cambridge University Press, 2001), p. 240.

46. In 1971-72, two Dutch commissions, one governmental and the other private, drew similar conclusions about drug policy: they found cannabis use to be a "relatively benign practice, generally limited to an adolescent phase of casual experimentation." They felt that the "gateway" theory regarding marijuana was actually due to the legal status of marijuana, which put cannabis users in contact with black-market dealers who also provided other, more dangerous substances. Both commissions stopped short of recommending legalization, but they did recommend decriminalization. In 1976 Minister of Health and Interior Irene Vorink, after reviewing medical and social studies on various drugs, determined that marijuana represented a much lower health risk than other illegal substances. Official policy did not legalize or decriminalize marijuana, but rather set laws with the greatest tolerance in Europe, and then recommended a policy of nonenforcement for marijuana laws due to its minimal risk to health. Sources: MacCoun and Reuter, *Drug War Heresies*, pp. 244-45; Ben Dronkers with Anne Bonney, "A History of Cannabis in

Holland," *Big Book of Buds* (California: Quick American Archives, 2001), p. 42.

47. "Because regulation is at the local level and is not entirely open, there is no official count of the number of coffeeshops in existence nationally." The number has declined from approximately 400 coffeeshops in Amsterdam since stricter laws were enacted in 1995 to an estimated 350 in 1998. (Source: MacCoun and Reuter, *Drug War Heresies*, p. 250.) In 1995, the Dutch government estimated that there were between 1,200 and 1,500 coffeeshops in the entire country. (Source: MacCoun and Reuter, *Drug War Heresies,* p. 241.) In 2001, the number of coffeeshops was estimated at 300 in Amsterdam, and a total of 900 throughout the Netherlands. (Source: Skip Stone, "The Dutch Coffeeshop Scene," *Big Book of Buds* (California: Quick American Archives, 2001), p. 163.)

48. "[T]he Harm Reduction concept has spread very fast in recent years and has now become the basis for a rational and pragmatic drug policy in almost every European Union country and several others like Australia, New Zealand, Canada, and Brazil." Source: Martin Jelsma, "Diverging Trends in International Drug Policy Making," Transnational Institute Drug Policy Paper (Sept. 2002).

49. In September 2002, Canada's special Senate Committee on Illegal Drugs released its final report on marijuana, stating that marijuana was substantially less harmful than alcohol, and recommended legalizing marijuana and clearing the record of anyone who had been convicted on marijuana possession charges. Source: "Pot less harmful than alcohol: Senate Report," CBC News Online (Sept. 5, 2002).
http://cbc.ca/stories/2002/09/04/pot_senate020904 [Dec. 2002].
For further information, which is regularly updated, see Lisa Khoo, "Canada's Marijuana Laws: The Debate over Decriminalization," CBC News Online (May 2002).
http://cbc.ca/news/indepth/background/marijuana_legalize.html [Dec. 2002].

50. Roland R. Griffiths and Geoffrey K. Mumford, "Caffeine: A Drug of

Abuse?" *Psychopharmacology–The 4th Generation of Progress,* a web publication of the American College of Neuropsychopharmacology. http://www.acnp.org/G4/GN401000165/CH161.html [Dec. 2002].

51. Peter Jaret, "Bottoms up for Health? Guidelines for Alcohol Consumption Remain Controversial," CNN website, health section (March 2000). http://www.cnn.com/2000/HEALTH/03/01/alcohol.health.wmd/index.html [Dec. 2002].

52. According to National Highway Traffic Safety Administration (NHTSA) statistics, 1.5 million drivers, or 1 out of every 120 licensed drivers in the U.S., was arrested in 1999 for drunk driving. (Source: NHTSA, National Center for Statistics & Analysis, Research & Development; Traffic Safety Facts 2000, Alcohol. DOT HS 809 323.) Many studies have established the link between alcohol and violence. In over 3 million crimes each year, the offender had been drinking. (Source: U.S. DOJ, BJS, "Alcohol and Crime," NCJ168632 (April 1998).)

53. King James I of England, "Counterblaste to Tobacco." (1604), can be viewed online at http://www.la.utexas.edu/research/poltheory/james/blaste/ [Dec. 2002].

54. Tobacco accounts for one in five deaths. Smoking-related illnesses cost the U.S. $150 billion annually. (Source: Centers for Disease Control and Prevention, "Targeting Tobacco Use: The Nation's Leading Cause of Death," 2002. http://www.cdc.gov/nccdphp/aag/aag_osh.htm [Dec. 2002].) Seventy percent of current cigarette smokers reported that they wanted to quit, and more than 40 percent had tried to quit at some point in the previous year. (Source: Centers for Disease Control and Prevention, "Cigarette Smoking Among Adults–United States, 2000" 51:29 (July 26, 2002), pp. 642-45.) http://www.cdc.gov/mmwr/preview/mmwrhtml/mm5129a3.htm [Dec. 2002].

55. "There are no confirmed cases of human deaths from cannabis poisoning in the world medical literature. [A] lethal dose in humans could

not be very easily achieved by smoking or ingesting the drug." (Source: W. Hall, R. Room, and S. Bondy, "WHO Project on Health Implications of Cannabis Use: A Comparative Appraisal of the Health and Psychological Consequences of Alcohol, Cannabis, Nicotine and Opiate Use," World Health Organization (WHO), Geneva, Switzerland (Aug. 28, 1995).

http://www.druglibrary.org/schaffer/hemp/general/who-index.htm [Dec. 2002].) Reporting on the suppressed WHO document, *The New Scientist* reported "not only that the amount of dope smoked worldwide does less harm to public health than drink and cigarettes, but that the same is likely to hold true even if people consumed dope on the same scale as these legal substances." (Source: "Marijuana Special Report: High Anxieties," *New Scientist* (Feb. 21, 1998).

http://www.newscientist.com/hottopics/marijuana/news.jsp [Dec. 2002].)

56. "Marijuana use in a prepaid health care–based study cohort had little effect on non-AIDS mortality in men and on total mortality in women." (Source: Sidney S. Beck, et al., "Marijuana Use and Mortality," *American Journal of Public Health* 87:4. (Apr. 1997), pp. 585-90.

http://www.ncbi.nlm.nih.gov/entrez/query.fcgi?cmd=Retrieve&db=PubMed &list_uids=9146436&dopt=Abstract [Dec. 2002].) "Marijuana is unique among illegal drugs in its political symbolism, its safety, and its wide use. More than 65 million Americans have tried marijuana, the use of which is not associated with increased mortality," J.G. Annas, "Reefer Madness—The Federal Response to California's Medical-Marijuana Law," *New England Journal of Medicine*, 337:6 (Aug. 7, 1997), pp. 435-439.

57. FBI Uniform Crime Reports, "Crime in the United States—2001."

58. Ibid.

59. The British Home Affairs Select Committee chairman, Chris Mullin, has said, "Attempts to combat illegal drugs by means of law enforcement have proved so manifestly unsuccessful that it is difficult to argue for the status quo." The report by the committee that Mullin chaired concluded that "if there is any single lesson from the experience of the

last 30 years, it is that policies based wholly or mainly on enforcement are destined to fail." Source: Jelsma, "Diverging Trends in International Drug Policy Making."

10 How to Legalize Marijuana

1. Samantha Sanchez, "Average Contributor Size in State Legislative Races," The National Institute on Money in State Politics (July 2, 1999). http://www.followthemoney.org/issues/contribsize.html [Dec. 2000]. Sanchez's research indicated that less than 1 percent of the population contributes to state office races. However, contributions to organizations with large lobbying or Political Action Committee arms and to national political campaigns, or to issue-driven elections, such as propositions, pushes the percentage higher. Still, it's a very small minority.